Rome 2025 Jubilee Year Travel Guide

Unique Experiences, Unmissable Events, Unfailing Grace
Authentic Rome Sites, Inspiring Walking Tours, Must-See
Destinations and Insider Tips for the Jubilee Year

Katerina Ferrara

IMMERSION TRAVEL PUBLISHING

ISBN: (Paperback) 979-8-9915871-4-3

ISBN: (eBook) 979-8-9915871-3-6

DISCLAIMER

The author is not a travel agent. All opinions, experiences, and views expressed by the author are based on my personal travel experiences. Businesses and websites recommended in this book may change ownership, rebrand, or close through no fault of the author. The author has received no compensation or sponsorship from any recommended business.

Contents

Explore More and Stay Connected!   VI

1. Introduction to the Jubilee Year   1

2. A Concise History of Rome   9

3. Arrive and Explore   24

4. What to Expect During a Jubilee Year   31

5. Opening of the Holy Doors   37

6. Booking Accommodation in Rome   40

7. The Papal Bull   45

8. Your Key to the Jubilee Year 2025   48

9. Centro Pellegrini   51

10. Jubilees Through the Centuries   54

11. Giro delle Sette Chiese   84

12. Visiting the Tomb of Saint Peter   108

13. Walking Tour: From Markets to Mosaics   112

14. Ancient Rome Walking Tour   126

15. Rome's Architectural Evolution Walking Tour   132

16. Holy Week and Easter during the Jubilee Year   142

17. Securing Tickets for Rome's Busiest Sites   162

18. Visiting the Catacombs of Rome   170

19. Shopping in Rome   177

20. Rome's Artistic Titans   181

21. Volunteering in the Spirit of the Jubilee   199

22. Calendar of Events Jubilee 2025   201

23. Taste of Rome   274

24. Accommodation Detail   285

25. Flexible and Walkable Itineraries   292

26. Reflections on the Jubilee Year   302

27. Select Bibliography   305

Endnotes

Thank You & Please Leave a Review   306

Connect with Me   308

Katerina Ferrara   311

Explore More and Stay Connected!

Thank you for joining me on this journey through the wonders of Italy.

Allow me to be your personal guide, sharing insider tips, unique experiences, and essential information to uncover the treasures of Italy like never before.

Sign up for my newsletter today and receive your **FREE downloadable guides** filled with curated itineraries, expert advice, and practical tips to make your adventures across Italy unforgettable and stress-free!

Scan Here

With your complimentary subscription, you'll enjoy:

- Monthly updates with insider secrets for Italy, top experiences, hidden spots, and seasonal highlights

- VIP access to exclusive offers on festival tours, events, and limited-time promotions

---

Travel Italy Book Series

Available now:

Book 1: *Ultimate Festival & Travel Guide Sicily*

Book 2: *Rome 2025 Jubilee Year Travel Guide*

Arriving in 2025:

Book 3: *Ultimate Festival & Travel Guide Rome and Beyond*

Book 4: *Ultimate Festival & Travel Guide Puglia*

Don't miss out on exclusive insights and bonus content to enhance your Italian journey! Sign up today and let's start exploring!

CHAPTER ONE

Introduction to the Jubilee Year

L'anno Santo

L'anno Santo, the Holy Year, is a significant event in the Catholic Church. It attracts millions of pilgrims to Rome. The year 2025 marks the next Jubilee, with the theme "Pilgrims of Hope". Its celebrations will officially begin in December 2024. This sacred event occurs every 25 years and offers pilgrims the opportunity to receive special indulgences through acts of faith, penance, and devotion.

Origins and Historical Background

The tradition of the Jubilee Year traces its origins to ancient Jewish customs. In the Old Testament, a "jubilee" was declared every 50 years when slaves were freed, debts were forgiven, and the land returned to its original owners. This biblical practice of renewal and mercy inspired the Catholic version, which was first instituted by Pope Boniface VIII in 1300.

Pope Boniface VIII declared the first Christian Jubilee in response to a growing number of pilgrims traveling to Rome to visit sacred sites. He proclaimed that any Christian who visited the Basilicas of St. Peter and St. Paul confessed their sins and performed certain religious acts during the Jubilee would receive a plenary indulgence, a remission of all temporal punishment for sin.

Initially planned as a once-in-a-century event, the Jubilee's triumph prompted later popes to shorten the interval to every 25 years, ensuring each generation's participation in this special time of grace and forgiveness.

Evolution of the Jubilee Year

Over the centuries, the Jubilee Year has evolved both in terms of spiritual significance and the scope of its celebrations. Some jubilees have been extraordinary, declared outside of the regular 25-year cycle, often to mark special occasions or to bring about spiritual renewal during times of crisis. For instance, Pope John Paul II declared the Great Jubilee of 2000 to usher in the new millennium and celebrate the 2000th anniversary of Christ's birth.

Specific rituals mark each Jubilee Year, the most iconic of which is the opening of the Holy Doors (Porta Sancta) at the four major basilicas in Rome—St. Peter's Basilica, St. John Lateran, St. Paul Outside the Walls, and St. Mary Major. These doors remain sealed during ordinary times and are only opened during a Jubilee Year, symbolizing the "extraordinary path" that leads to salvation. Pilgrims passing through these Holy Doors are granted indulgences, signifying the forgiveness of sins.

Jubilee of 2025

The theme "Pilgrims of Hope" reflects a global call for unity, mercy, and renewal, focusing on the Church's mission of bringing hope and healing to the world.

Rome will become the center of worldwide attention, as millions of pilgrims are expected to flock to the city to take part in the spiritual events planned for the year. The Vatican will organize religious services, special masses, catechesis, and cultural events. Many of the most iconic sites in Rome, including the Vatican Museums, St. Peter's Square, and the Roman basilicas, will be central to the celebrations.

In the aftermath of the trials brought about by the pandemic years, the 2025 Jubilee gains significance in showcasing hope, recovery, and a rejuvenated sense of global community and faith. In a nod to modern times, the Vatican has introduced the Carta del Pellegrino. This digital pilgrimage card will help manage the flow of pilgrims and provide access to various services.

The celebration is expected to be a transformative event, blending centuries-old traditions with modern approaches. Specific expectations include:

- Enhanced use of technology, including virtual pilgrimages and digital resources, to make the Jubilee more accessible globally.

- Special events and initiatives addressing contemporary social issues align with Pope Francis's emphasis on social justice and mercy.

- Increased interfaith dialogue and ecumenical events, promoting unity and understanding among different faiths.

Cultural Significance of the Jubilee

Beyond its religious importance, the holy year holds immense cultural significance. It catalyzes artistic expression, with many artists, musicians, and performers creating works inspired by the Jubilee themes. The event also boosts cultural tourism, allowing visitors to experience Rome's deep-rooted history and artistic heritage. The event often spurs preservation efforts for historical sites and artworks, leaving a lasting cultural legacy.

Global Impact of the Jubilee

Though centered in Rome, the Jubilee's impact resonates across the world. Local churches across the globe will organize parallel events, creating a sense of universal participation. The message of hope and renewal is expected to inspire social and charitable initiatives far beyond Rome's borders. The global media's attention on the celebration provides an opportunity for the Church to address worldwide issues and promote its message of peace and solidarity on an international stage.

Preparations in Rome

Rome is undergoing extensive preparations. The event is expected to draw millions of pilgrims from around the world. Major projects include key infrastructure improvements, such as the transformation of Piazza Pia into a pedestrian-friendly space that will seamlessly link Castel Sant'Angelo and St. Peter's Square. This redevelopment includes the construction of new underpasses to manage traffic flow more effectively, making the site safer and more accessible for the expected influx of visitors. Beyond the immediate vicinity of the Vatican, significant investments are being made to upgrade roads, public transport systems, and tourist facilities throughout the city.

One of the most notable developments near Piazza Pia is an archaeological excavation that has uncovered significant ancient Roman ruins, including a fullonica—an ancient Roman laundry facility. This discovery provides an exciting glimpse into the daily life and industrial activities of Roman citizens, showing how textiles were cleaned and processed in Roman times. Despite the complexity of preserving such historically important sites, construction remains on schedule, with plans to complete the project by the end of 2024, ensuring that the city's modern development aligns with its rich history.

My friends who live in Rome as it prepares for the 2025 special events are complaining about closed streets and construction "dappertutto" (everywhere). While locals insist the work won't be finished in time, history suggests otherwise. No doubt Roman citizens have voiced these same concerns before every Jubilee since 1300, as popes and city leaders pushed construction teams to their limits, determined to present Rome in its most magnificent state to welcome millions of visitors.

Preparations for the Jubilee extend far beyond infrastructure. Rome is enhancing key religious sites, improving pedestrian routes to accommodate the sizeable crowds, and upgrading public transportation to handle the increased demand.

Comprehensive security measures are also being implemented to ensure the safety of the millions of pilgrims and tourists expected during the event. In the hospitality sector, hotels, restaurants, and tourist services are expanding their capacity and training staff to cater to the diverse needs of international visitors.

International collaborations are another key aspect of the preparations, with the Vatican working closely with governments and organizations worldwide to streamline pilgrim travel and ensure a smooth experience for visitors from across the globe. These combined efforts aim to create a harmonious blend of ancient heritage, modern convenience, and warm hospitality as the city gears up for this once-in-a-lifetime spiritual event.

How to Use this Guide

Whether you're a pilgrim seeking spiritual renewal or a traveler eager to experience the best of the Eternal City, this guide is designed to help you maximize your Jubilee Year journey. It's structured to provide practical advice, detailed itineraries, and insights into both the spiritual and cultural richness of Rome.

Jubilee Year Essentials: We will begin with a comprehensive overview, focusing on its religious significance, key events, and the central role of the Holy Doors at Rome's four major basilicas—St. Peter's, St. John Lateran, St. Mary Major, and St. Paul Outside the Walls. This section provides essential information on how to obtain indulgences, a schedule of major liturgical events, and valuable tips for navigating the crowds during peak periods. Whether you're attending Mass at the basilicas or walking through the Holy Doors, this section ensures you're prepared for these important spiritual milestones.

The Giro delle Sette Chiese: We will explore the revived traditional pilgrimage route that leads you through Rome's most sacred sites. Our guide includes a detailed itinerary for the Giro delle Sette Chiese, offering both historical context and practical advice for walking the route. You'll find step-by-step guidance, along with insider tips on pacing yourself, whether you plan to complete the pilgrimage in one day or over several. This journey connects you to centuries of devotion and brings a deeply enriching spiritual experience.

Walking Tours of Rome: Rome is best discovered on foot, and our walking tours are tailored to help you uncover the city's top attractions while soaking in its rich history and vibrant culture. These tours are designed to complement your Jubilee experience, guiding you to iconic landmarks such as the Colosseum, Roman Forum, and Pantheon, while also revealing hidden churches, quiet piazzas, and stunning fountains. Each tour provides logical steps through the city, ideal stops for rest and refreshment, and fascinating facts to enhance your exploration of the city.

Top Sites and Hidden Gems: For those looking to balance Rome's famous sites with off-the-beaten-path discoveries, this section offers a mix of both. From the grandeur of Vatican City to the charming streets of Trastevere, you'll find recommendations for visiting the must-see monuments along with tips on discovering more intimate, often overlooked corners of the city. Whether it's a hidden chapel or a tucked-away café, this section invites you to experience a more personal side of Rome.

Practical Information and Tips: With millions of visitors expected for the Jubilee Year, careful planning is essential. These sections cover everything you need to know, from securing tickets for key events to the best times to visit popular sites and how to avoid long lines. I provide practical advice on transportation, accommodations, and navigating Rome's public transport system. Whether you're a first-time visitor or a seasoned traveler, these tips will keep your journey smooth and stress-free.

Enhancing Your Spiritual Journey: Beyond the logistics, this guide emphasizes the deeper, spiritual aspects of the Jubilee. Here, you'll find suggestions on how to deepen your personal journey during this holy year. We offer ideas for visiting spiritually significant sites, engaging in acts of charity, and enriching your pilgrimage experience in ways that will stay with you long after you leave Rome. This section helps turn your journey into not just a trip, but a transformative experience.

Itineraries: This book offers itinerary ideas for three, five or eight nights in Rome. With these itineraries, you'll discover the beauty and vibrancy of Rome while making the most of your Jubilee experience. Whether you're a seasoned traveler or a first-time visitor, we invite you to embark on this extraordinary journey through one of the world's most captivating cities.

Partner this Guide: If you plan to explore beyond Rome, consider pairing this guide with my Ultimate Festival & Travel Guide Rome and Beyond book, which offers itineraries in the city and also and insights into other cities nearby and easy day trips outside of Rome. (Arriving on Amazon March 2025).

This guide is comprehensive yet adaptable, designed to be a flexible companion throughout your Jubilee Year pilgrimage. Whether you follow it page by page or skip to the sections that interest you most, it's meant to accompany you through Rome's historic streets and help you experience the rich cultural and spiritual offerings this extraordinary year brings.

Keep it handy as you plan and reflect—safe travels, and may your journey be filled with grace, renewal, and unforgettable moments!

CHAPTER TWO

A Concise History of Rome

From Rome's Founding to Present Day

S ummarizing Rome's history concisely is impossible, but I'll attempt it. Rome, known as "The Eternal City," has a history that spans over 2,500 years, making it one of the oldest continuously inhabited cities in the world. Its history is a tapestry of mythology, legendary figures, and monumental events that have shaped Western civilization.

The Importance of Knowing Rome's History for Pilgrims

Visiting Rome as a pilgrim offers not just a spiritual journey but a deeper connection to the city's sacred and historical significance. Understanding Rome's rich history allows you to fully appreciate the layers of meaning behind its monumental sites, ancient churches, and religious traditions.

By knowing the stories of the past, you gain a greater sense of awe and reverence as you walk the same streets where emperors, saints, and martyrs once lived.

As a pilgrim, having knowledge of Rome's history enriches your experience by offering context to the relics you venerate, the churches you visit, and the rituals you participate in. When you stand before St. Peter's Basilica or walk through the Roman Forum, you're not just a traveler admiring architecture; you're a participant in a long, continuous thread of history that connects you to generations of believers and historical figures. This awareness turns each site into a profound spiritual and intellectual encounter, deepening your connection with the city and enhancing your pilgrimage journey.

Myth of Romulus and Remus

According to Roman mythology, Rome was founded in 753 BC by Romulus, who, along with his twin brother Remus, was said to have been raised by a she-wolf. The story of their upbringing is one of the most enduring legends of Rome's beginnings, symbolizing the city's strength and resilience. Romulus later killed Remus in a dispute over the location of the new city and became its first king, giving Rome its name. This myth highlights Rome's early association with divine favor and violence, which would shape its cultural identity for centuries to come.

The Roman Kingdom (753-509 BC)

Rome began as a small city-state ruled by a series of kings, with Romulus as its legendary first monarch. The early Roman kingdom focused on consolidating power over neighboring tribes and establishing the foundations of Roman society. During this period, the Roman Senate, a council of elders, was established to advise the kings and would later play a significant role in the Republic and Empire. The city's first major public works, including temples and drainage systems like the Cloaca Maxima, were also constructed during this time, laying the groundwork for Rome's expansion into a larger political entity.

Republican Governance (509-27 BC)

In 509 BC, Rome transitioned from monarchy to a republic following the overthrow of its last king, Tarquin the Proud. The establishment of the Roman Republic was a pivotal moment in the city's history, as it developed a complex system of governance with checks and balances. The consuls, who were elected annually, shared power with the Senate and other elected officials. This period also saw the creation of key legal principles, including Roman law, which would later influence legal systems worldwide. The Republic expanded Rome's influence throughout Italy through alliances and military conquests.

Military Conquests (509-27 BC)

The Republic was marked by significant military campaigns, including the Punic Wars against Carthage (264-146 BC), which solidified Rome's dominance over the western Mediterranean. Rome's victory over Hannibal in the Second Punic War allowed for further expansion, including the annexation of Spain and North Africa.

The conquest of Greece and Macedonia in the 2nd century BC brought Greek culture, philosophy, and art into Roman life, leaving a lasting impact on the Roman intellectual and artistic traditions. By the end of the Republic, Rome had become the most powerful state in the Mediterranean, with territories stretching from Gaul to Egypt.

The Roman Empire (27 BC - AD 476)

Augustus and the Pax Romana

In 27 BC, following years of civil war, Octavian, later known as Augustus, became the first Roman emperor, marking the beginning of the Roman Empire. His reign ushered in the Pax Romana, a period of relative peace and prosperity that lasted for over two centuries.

Augustus reformed the military, created an efficient administrative system, and initiated vast building projects that transformed Rome into a city of marble. During this period, literature and the arts flourished under figures like Virgil, Horace, and Ovid, contributing to Rome's cultural golden age.

Expansion and Architectural Achievements

The Empire reached its greatest territorial extent under Emperor Trajan in the early 2nd century AD, stretching from Britain in the west to Mesopotamia in the east. Rome itself became a city of monumental architecture, with structures such as the Colosseum, Pantheon, and Trajan's Column being constructed. These projects showcased Roman engineering prowess, with innovations like aqueducts, paved roads, and public baths being spread across the empire. The city became the political and cultural center of a vast empire that connected Europe, Africa, and the Near East.

Christianity and Constantine

By the 4th century AD, Christianity, which had initially been persecuted under several emperors, became the dominant religion of the Roman Empire. Emperor Constantine the Great played a crucial role in this transformation, particularly with the Edict of Milan in AD 313, which legalized Christianity.

Constantine's conversion to Christianity is often attributed to a dramatic event in AD 312, the night before the Battle of the Milvian Bridge. According to legend, Constantine had a vision of a cross in the sky accompanied by the words "In this sign, you will conquer" (In hoc signo vinces). He subsequently adopted the Christian symbol and won the battle, a victory that secured his position as the ruler of the Western Roman Empire.

Constantine also moved the empire's capital to Byzantium, renaming it Constantinople (modern-day Istanbul), marking the beginning of a shift in power from Rome to the east. This shift left a power vacuum in Rome, where the popes gradually began assuming more political and civic leadership in the city.

As the imperial focus moved away from Rome, the papacy took on a greater role not only in spiritual matters but also in governing the city. Pope Sylvester I is traditionally credited with collaborating with Constantine in many of these projects. Constantine's reign also oversaw the construction of significant Christian sites in Rome, including St. Peter's Basilica, solidifying the city's central place in Christendom and establishing the pope's influence over its religious and civic life.

The Fall of the Western Roman Empire (AD 476)

Decline and Division

By the 5th century, the Western Roman Empire faced numerous challenges, including economic decline, administrative corruption, and invasions by barbarian tribes such as the Visigoths and Vandals. In AD 476, the last Roman emperor of the West, Romulus Augustulus, was deposed by the Germanic chieftain Odoacer, marking the traditional date for the fall of the Western Roman Empire.

Although Rome fell, many of its institutions, cultural practices, and architectural innovations persisted in the East.

The Eastern Roman Empire (Byzantine Empire)

Despite the collapse of the West, the Eastern Roman Empire, known later as the Byzantine Empire, continued to thrive for nearly a millennium. It's important to note that the people of this empire did not refer to themselves as Byzantines; they considered themselves Romans, and the empire as a continuation of the Roman state. The term "Byzantine Empire" was coined by later historians to differentiate it from the earlier Roman Empire, emphasizing the cultural and political distinctions that developed over time.

Its capital, Constantinople, became a center of Christian scholarship, art, and commerce. The Byzantine Empire preserved much of Roman law and culture while developing its own unique identity, until its eventual fall to the Ottoman Turks in 1453.

Medieval Rome and the Papal States

The Middle Ages

After the fall of the Western Roman Empire in 476 AD, Rome's influence significantly waned, and the city fell into a prolonged period of decline, becoming part of the Papal States governed by the Pope. Throughout the Middle Ages, Rome faced numerous challenges, including invasions by the Visigoths in 410 AD and the Vandals in 455 AD, which devastated the city. These invasions led to repeated plundering and destruction, leaving many ancient buildings in ruins.

By the 9th and 10th centuries, Rome was a shadow of its former glory. Large sections of the city were abandoned, and many of its iconic monuments had either decayed or been repurposed. The Colosseum, for example, was used as a fortress by local baronial families, while ancient temples were stripped of their marble and other valuable materials to build new churches and fortifications. The city's population, which had once reached over a million during the height of the Roman Empire, dwindled to a mere fraction, with some estimates suggesting it dropped to fewer than 50,000 inhabitants.

Medieval Rome also suffered from political instability, with power struggles between the papacy, local aristocratic families (such as the powerful Orsini and Colonna families), and foreign rulers like the Holy Roman Emperors. The city, once the center of an empire, was now marked by factional violence, lawlessness, and a lack of centralised authority. The urban infrastructure had fallen into disrepair, and extensive areas of the city were essentially left in ruins.

While Rome remained a spiritual center due to the presence of the papacy, its political and cultural importance had significantly diminished. Even the establishment of the Holy Roman Empire in 800 AD, when Charlemagne was crowned emperor in St. Peter's Basilica, could not fully revive the city's stature. Although this coronation reinforced Rome's status as the spiritual heart of Western Christendom, the city itself continued to face internal disputes and external threats.

The Avignon Papacy (1309-1377) exacerbated Rome's decline further. For nearly 70 years, the papacy was moved from Rome to Avignon in southern France, largely due to political pressures and instability in Italy. During this period, seven successive popes ruled from Avignon, and Rome fell into further neglect. With the papal court and its associated wealth and influence gone, many of the city's churches, public buildings, and infrastructure decayed even further. The absence of the Pope also led to economic decline, as Rome was no longer the primary destination for pilgrims or a center of Catholic power.

After nearly seven decades, Pope Gregory XI finally returned the papacy to Rome in 1377, marking the end of the Avignon Papacy. Even so, the damage to the city had been significant, and its recovery would take centuries. The return of the papacy did not immediately restore Rome's political or economic power, and the city remained in a fragile state leading into the Renaissance.

Renaissance Rome

By the 14th century, Rome was in desperate need of revival, both physically and culturally. The Renaissance brought that renewal, particularly under the leadership of the Popes, who became great patrons of the arts. Rome's transformation began in earnest during the 15th century, as the popes, including Pope Nicholas V and Pope Julius II, launched massive building and restoration projects. These efforts sought to return Rome to its former glory and establish it as the center of the Christian world once more.

During the Renaissance, Rome flourished as a center of art, culture, and scholarship. The construction of the new St. Peter's Basilica, the decoration of the Sistine Chapel, and the commissioning of works by artists like Michelangelo, Raphael, and Bernini symbolized this cultural and spiritual renewal.

The city became a magnet for artists, architects, and scholars from across Europe, reclaiming its place as both a religious and artistic capital. As the papacy strengthened its influence, Renaissance Rome emerged from its medieval decay to become a beacon of artistic innovation and religious power.

Baroque Rome (17th Century)

Following the Renaissance, Rome continued to thrive during the Baroque period (17th century), a time marked by grandeur and dramatic artistic expression. The Baroque Popes, such as Pope Urban VIII and Pope Innocent X, commissioned magnificent works that emphasized the power and glory of the Catholic Church.

Bernini's Colonnade

Gian Lorenzo Bernini, the master of Baroque architecture and sculpture, left an indelible mark on the city with masterpieces such as the Colonnade of St. Peter's Square, the Fountain of the Four Rivers in Piazza Navona, and the grand Baldacchino over the high altar of St. Peter's Basilica.

Bernini's Colonnade

The Trevi Fountain

During this period, Rome became a symbol of the Catholic Counter-Reformation, with art and architecture designed to inspire faith and devotion.

The city was adorned with grand churches, elaborate fountains, and opulent palaces, creating a theatrical, awe-inspiring atmosphere that sought to display the spiritual and political dominance of the papacy. Commissioned by Pope Clement XII, the construction of the Trevi Fountain began in 1732 and was completed in 1762, standing today as a stunning example of Baroque artistry.

Trevi Fountain

Napoleonic Era and Restoration

Rome's fortunes shifted dramatically in the late 18th and early 19th centuries when it fell under the control of Napoleon Bonaparte. In 1809, Napoleon annexed the Papal States and declared Rome part of the French Empire, exiling Pope Pius VII to France. During his exile, Pope Pius VII was held in various locations, including Fontainebleau, but this exile was not akin to the earlier Avignon Papacy (1309–1377), when the papacy officially moved its seat to Avignon in southern France for nearly 70 years.

While the Pope was in exile under Napoleon, Rome was plundered, and many of its most precious treasures were looted and sent to Paris. Napoleon's forces seized many artworks, religious artifacts, and historical items, stripping Rome of some of its most valued cultural heritage. These items were displayed in Paris, most notably in the Louvre, symbolizing France's dominance over the once-mighty capital of Christendom.

Besides the loss of treasures, many of Rome's churches, palaces, and public buildings fell into disrepair, and the city endured years of neglect under foreign rule. However, after Napoleon's defeat in 1814, the Congress of Vienna restored the Papal States, and Pope Pius VII returned to Rome, reestablishing the city as the spiritual center of Catholicism. His return marked the end of French control and the restoration of Rome's religious leadership. Efforts were made to repair the damage and recover some of the looted treasures, though many valuable items remained in France.

During this period of restoration, Rome remained an important religious center but was politically fragmented and lacked the same influence it had held during the Renaissance and Baroque periods. Nonetheless, the papacy continued to commission important works of art and architecture, ensuring that the city retained its cultural significance and slowly rebuilt its prominence as the heart of the Catholic world.

Modern Rome

Unification of Italy

The 19th century was a pivotal era for Rome, as it became the focal point of the Italian unification movement, also known as the Risorgimento. The movement sought to unite the various states and territories of the Italian Peninsula, which had long been divided into small kingdoms, duchies, and the Papal States. Leading figures like Giuseppe Garibaldi, Count Cavour, and King Victor Emmanuel II played key roles in the struggle to create a unified Italian nation.

Before Rome became the capital of Italy, several cities served as the political center for the newly formed Kingdom of Italy. Turin (Torino), the capital of the Kingdom of Sardinia, became the first capital of the unified Kingdom of Italy in 1861, following the proclamation of Victor Emmanuel II as the first King of Italy. However, the capital was soon moved to Florence in 1865 as part of a political agreement aimed at placating various factions within the new kingdom and maintaining good relations with France, which was then protecting the Papal States from potential attacks.

Despite Florence's status as the capital, Rome was seen as the ultimate and symbolic choice due to its historical, cultural, and religious significance. However, the Pope ruled Rome and the surrounding Papal States. The Papal States were protected by French troops under Napoleon III, which prevented Italian forces from taking Rome by force.

This situation changed in 1870, when the outbreak of the Franco-Prussian War forced France to withdraw its troops from Rome. With no French protection, the Kingdom of Italy seized the opportunity, and Italian troops led by General Raffaele Cadorna entered Rome on September 20, 1870, breaching the Aurelian Walls at Porta Pia after a short skirmish. This event, known as the Capture of Rome, effectively ended the Pope's temporal rule over the city.

In 1871, Rome was formally declared the capital of the Kingdom of Italy, marking the culmination of the Risorgimento. The Pope, Pius IX, refused to recognize the new Italian state and declared himself a "prisoner" within the Vatican, refusing to leave the Vatican grounds in protest. This situation, known as the "Roman Question," persisted for decades until the Lateran Treaty of 1929, which established Vatican City as an independent sovereign state, formally resolving the tension between the Papacy and the Italian government.

Rome's new role as Italy's capital sparked significant modernization efforts. The city underwent major urban development to accommodate its new political role, including the construction of public buildings, infrastructure, and transportation systems.

However, Rome's transition to the capital was not without challenges. The integration of the city into the modern Italian state required balancing its ancient history and religious significance with the needs of a growing urban population. Nevertheless, Rome's status as the capital of Italy solidified its place at the heart of Italian national identity, becoming both a political center and a symbol of the country's unity and heritage.

20th Century to Present

Rome, like the rest of Italy, was deeply affected by the two world wars of the 20th century. While the city itself was not a major battleground during World War I, the conflict had far-reaching economic and social impacts on the Italian nation, including Rome. Italy's involvement in World War I (1915-1918) put a significant strain on its economy, leading to food shortages, inflation, and general unrest in the aftermath of the war.

Though Rome escaped direct damage, the city, along with the rest of the country, faced significant hardship as it grappled with the consequences of war.

In World War II, Rome played a much more direct role in the conflict. Under the dictatorship of Benito Mussolini and his Fascist regime, Italy aligned itself with Nazi Germany. Rome became an important administrative center for the Fascist government, and many of its political and military decisions were made within the city's borders. However, as the war turned against the Axis powers, Rome came under increasing threat.

By 1943, after the fall of Mussolini and Italy's surrender to the Allied forces, Rome was occupied by German forces. The occupation led to harsh reprisals against the local population and the persecution of Roman Jews. The 1943 deportation of the Jewish community from Rome's Ghetto to Nazi concentration camps remains one of the darkest moments in the city's modern history. Rome also experienced several Allied air raids during the war, though, compared to other Italian cities, it was spared from total destruction due to its vast cultural and religious significance. The Vatican's diplomatic status also helped shield parts of the city, but many neighborhoods suffered from bombings, with key infrastructure, such as railways and bridges, being targeted.

One of the most significant moments came in June 1944, when Rome was liberated by the Allied forces under General Mark Clark. Rome became the first major European capital to be liberated from Nazi control, marking a turning point in Italy's path towards post-war recovery. The city emerged from World War II physically damaged and economically devastated, but its architectural and cultural heritage was largely preserved.

Liberation Day in Italy, known as Festa della Liberazione is celebrated annually on April 25, not in June. This national holiday marks the liberation of Italy from Nazi occupation and Fascist rule during World War II. It commemorates the end of the Italian Civil War and the victory of the Italian resistance movement in 1945.

Post-War Rome: A Metropolis Reborn

After the devastation of World War II, Rome entered a period of rapid reconstruction and expansion, particularly during the 1950s and 1960s. This post-war boom saw the city transform into a bustling metropolis and the heart of Italy's political and cultural life. It was during this period that Rome became a symbol of Italy's recovery, hosting major international events, including the 1960 Summer Olympics, which brought global attention to the city and further cemented its role as a center for diplomacy, art, and tourism.

As the capital of Italy, Rome continued to modernize, with new neighborhoods and infrastructure being built to accommodate the growing population. The city's role as the seat of the Roman Catholic Church continued to draw pilgrims and tourists alike, while its ancient ruins and Renaissance art became must-see destinations for travelers from around the world.

Rome's legacy remains vast, influencing language, law, architecture, engineering, and governance. The Latin language, Roman law, and Roman architectural styles have had a lasting impact on Western civilization. Today, Rome stands as a UNESCO World Heritage Site, attracting millions of visitors annually to its ancient ruins, Renaissance masterpieces, and vibrant modern culture. Its history is a testament to its resilience, and the city continues to be a symbol of Italy's enduring influence on world history.

CHAPTER THREE

Arrive and Explore

Airport, Transport, Tours, and Options

R ome is a city where history, culture, and spirituality converge, making it an incredible destination during the Jubilee Year. This section will help you arrive in Rome seamlessly, explore its vibrant center, and get around with ease.

Airport Information and Getting to the City Center

Rome has two main airports: Leonardo da Vinci–Fiumicino Airport (FCO), located 32 km (20 miles) from the city center, and Ciampino Airport (CIA), primarily serving low-cost airlines, situated 15 km (9 miles) from central Rome.

From Fiumicino Airport (FCO):

- Leonardo Express: A direct train from Fiumicino to Termini Station in the city center, running every 15-30 minutes. The journey takes about 32 minutes, costing around €14.

- Taxis: Official taxis have a flat rate to the center. Be sure to take the official white taxis, as unauthorized drivers may charge more.

- Shuttle Bus: Multiple shuttle bus companies operate between Fiumicino and various locations in central Rome. Prices range from €6 to €8, with services taking about an hour.

- Private Transfers: Pre-arranged transfers offer convenience, with services costing around €60-€80 for door-to-door travel.

From Ciampino Airport (CIA):

- Bus and Metro: Terravision or SIT shuttle buses connect Ciampino to Termini Station, with tickets costing around €6. The journey takes about 40 minutes.

- Taxi: A flat rate of €31 is charged for taxis to the center.

Why Stay in the Center of Rome?

If your budget can handle it, I strongly suggest you stay in Rome and not a suburb. Choosing accommodations in the historic center of Rome offers unmatched access to the city's principal attractions, dining options, and cultural activities.

The neighborhoods of Centro Storico, Trastevere, and Monti are ideal for visitors wanting to immerse themselves at the core of the Eternal City. This will allow you to walk early in the morning and late at night without worrying about public transport to arrive further afield. Staying in the center also gives you the option to return to your hotel for a siesta in the afternoon if needed.

- Walkability: Staying in the center allows you to explore Rome on foot, passing through narrow streets, piazzas, and famous sites like the Colosseum, the Pantheon, and St. Peter's Basilica.

- Access to Public Transport: Being centrally located ensures you are close to bus stops, metro stations, and even electric scooters for quick and convenient travel.

- Comfort: My last trip to Rome I walked 12 miles in one day, just seeing the sites. With a hotel in the center you have the option to return for a rest if the day is hot or you need a break.

- Cultural Immersion: Living among Rome's iconic sites lets you experience the city's vibrant culture, from dining at traditional trattorias to visiting famous landmarks early in the morning before the crowds.

Getting Around Rome

Navigating Rome is easy with various transportation options, making it simple to explore the city whether you're staying in the center or venturing to the outskirts.

Metro: Rome has three metro lines—A (orange), B (blue), and C (green)—that connect key areas of the city. Line A takes you to popular sites like the Spanish Steps and the Vatican, while Line B stops near the Colosseum. Tickets are affordable at €1.50 for 100 minutes of travel, with multi-day passes also available.

Bus and Tram: ATAC buses and trams offer comprehensive coverage of the city. While they can be slower during rush hours, they are useful for reaching areas not serviced by the metro. Metro tickets can be purchased at stations or newsstands.

Taxi: Official white taxis are available throughout the city. You can hail them on the street, or use apps like FreeNow, a taxi app that allows you to call a taxi with ease. Use authorized taxis, as they are metered, and you can avoid overcharging.

Uber: Although Uber operates in Rome, only the Uber Black service is available, meaning the prices are higher than standard taxis. Uber Black provides luxury vehicles and private drivers.

Electric Scooters and Bikes: Several companies provide electric scooters for rent. This eco-friendly option is great for quick trips through Rome's narrow streets.

Public Transport: Consider purchasing a Roma Pass (www.romapass.it), which offers access to public transport and free or discounted entry to many sites. It also allows skip-the-line access to some attractions.

Walking in Rome

Rome is often best experienced on foot. The compact nature of the historic center means many famous landmarks are within walking distance of one another. Wear comfortable shoes and prepare to explore hidden gems like quaint churches, charming cafes, and historical ruins that may not be on your original itinerary.

Not Able to Walk Long Distances?

If walking long distances isn't an option for you, but you still want to experience the best of Rome's incredible sights, consider exploring the city with a golf cart tour or tour by car. Ideal for those with mobility concerns or seeking a relaxed way to see top attractions without walking strain.

Golf Cart Tours in Rome provide an intimate and accessible way to visit iconic landmarks. Here's how it works:

- Comfort and Flexibility: You'll travel in a small, comfortable electric golf cart, perfect for navigating through Rome's narrow streets and crowded areas. The carts can easily access places that larger tour buses cannot, giving you a more personal and up-close experience of the city's treasures.

- Customized Itineraries: Many golf cart tours allow for customized itineraries, letting you prioritize the landmarks you want to see. Whether it's the Colosseum, the Roman Forum, Vatican City, or the Pantheon, you can arrange a tour that fits your pace and interests.

- Expert Guides: The tours come with knowledgeable guides who provide engaging commentary as you explore Rome's rich history and culture. They can share fascinating stories and facts while ensuring you don't miss any important details.

- Duration Options: Tours range from 2 to 4 hours, depending on how much you'd like to see. This means you can explore at your own pace, taking breaks as needed.

- Accessible for All: Golf cart tours are an excellent option for families with young children, elderly travelers, or anyone with mobility limitations. The smooth rides make them a convenient and enjoyable way to see Rome without physical exertion.

There are many tour companies offering this option. Here is one example: https://www.golfcarttours.it/

Knowing transportation options and staying in Rome's heart will maximize your time in this incredible city. Whether you prefer the convenience of the metro or the charm of walking through Rome's ancient streets, this guide will help you navigate with ease during your publicvisit.

Tour Guides versus Self Guided Tours

While self-guided walking tours offer flexibility and the chance to explore at your own pace, there's something unique about the insights provided by a local guide. A professional guide can offer historical context, local stories, and access to sites that might otherwise be unavailable to the general public.

Many visitors to Rome find that hiring a guide enhances their experience, especially in places with deep historical layers, like the Roman Forum or Vatican City. Booking a guide in advance is often a good idea, especially during peak times or for more specialized tours. For those who prefer self-guided options, audio tours and detailed maps are available, but keep in mind that a guide can provide a deeper connection to the city's rich history.

Here are some tour operators specific to Rome, offering a range of guided tours from historical and cultural experiences to specialized food and art tours:

1. **Walks of Italy:** Specializes in small group tours with expert guides, covering key sites like the Vatican, Colosseum, and more. Website: www.walksofitaly.com

2. **Rome Private Guides**: Offers private and small group tours with licensed guides, focusing on personalized experiences in Rome's major landmarks. www.romeprivateguides.com

3. **The Roman Guy:** A popular operator providing guided tours of iconic sites such as the Vatican Museums and the Colosseum. Website: www.theromanguy.com

4. **LivItaly Tours:** Known for intimate, small-group and private tours, LivItaly covers everything from the Vatican to immersive food experiences. Website: www.livitaly.com

5. **Dark Rome Tours**: Focuses on skip-the-line tours for Rome's must-see attractions, offering both daytime and after-hours experiences. Website: www.darkrome.com

6. **Eternal City Tours:** Specializes in Christian pilgrimages and cultural tours, exploring religious and historical sites throughout Rome. Website: www.eternalcitytours.com

7. **When In Rome Tours:** Provides detailed tours of Rome's ancient ruins, museums, and neighborhoods, with an emphasis on history and art. Website: www.wheninrometours.com

8. **Angel Tours:** Provides small group tours with a personal touch and even special art tours www.angeltours.eu

Each of these tour operators offers unique experiences that cater to different interests, from food and art to history and religion.

CHAPTER FOUR

What to Expect During a Jubilee Year

Busiest Weeks, Best Weeks, and Main Events

For visitors and pilgrims, the holy year offers a unique experience combining reflection, prayer, and spiritual growth with cultural and historical opportunities. During the Jubilee, Rome transforms into a city of devotion and celebration, with special events held throughout the year. It is important to understand both the religious and logistical aspects of what this momentous year entails, especially considering the millions of pilgrims expected to visit.

The 2025 Jubilee is expected to attract over 25 million pilgrims from around the world, with peak attendance during major religious events and Holy Week. This will significantly increase crowd sizes at key religious sites, so planning your visits accordingly will be essential. The busiest periods are likely to be Holy Week, Christmas, Easter, and the Feast of Saints Peter and

Paul at the end of June, when the number of visitors may reach its highest point.

- **Busiest Weeks:** Pilgrims should expect the weeks around Christmas, Easter, and major feast days to be the most crowded. Additionally, summer months will see a peak in tourism, when pilgrims and travelers alike flock to Rome. The months of April, May, and June leading up to the Feast of Saints Peter and Paul, one of the Jubilee's central moments, will likely see massive crowds, particularly in the areas around St. Peter's Basilica and other pilgrimage sites.

- **Opening of the Holy Doors:** The most important ritual of the Jubilee Year is the opening of the Holy Doors, signifying the beginning of the Jubilee. Pilgrims pass through the Holy Doors to receive indulgences, a practice rooted in the idea of physical movement reflecting a journey of the soul. The first of these doors to be opened will be at St. Peter's Basilica, with doors at St. John Lateran, St. Mary Major, and St. Paul Outside the Walls following suit.

- **Major Pilgrimage Sites:** Pilgrims are encouraged to visit Rome's four major basilicas: St. Peter's Basilica, St. John Lateran, St. Paul Outside the Walls, and St. Mary Major. Each of these holy sites will play a central role in the celebrations, hosting special masses, prayer services, and other religious events. Early arrival to these sites is recommended to avoid long waits, especially during peak weeks. See Practical Advice chapter for information and websites you can use to book in advance.

- **Special Masses and Events:** The Vatican will hold numerous masses, prayer services, and catechetical sessions for pilgrims.

Each of Rome's basilicas will host daily religious activities, while cultural events, exhibitions, and concerts will complement the spiritual celebrations. Visitors can expect a variety of enriching experiences that offer insight into Rome's rich religious and cultural heritage.

- **Indulgences:** Pilgrims who visit the four basilicas, pass through the Holy Doors, and partake in the sacraments of confession, the Eucharist, and prayers for the Pope's intentions can receive a plenary indulgence. This is a rare opportunity that draws Catholics from around the world, making the Jubilee Year a significant moment of grace.

- **The Transformation of Rome:** Throughout the Jubilee Year, Rome will transform into a city of pilgrimage. Jubilee symbols will adorn streets, squares, and churches. Many chances to engage in both spiritual and cultural activities will be available. From the Vatican to the Roman Forum, visitors will see the city bustling with devotion and excitement as it welcomes millions of pilgrims.

Best Weeks to Visit (Lowest Volume Periods):

- **January** (Post-New Year through Mid-February): After the Christmas and New Year's celebrations, Rome typically sees a dip in tourism. The colder winter months are quieter, and while there may still be pilgrims, the overall volume will be much lower compared to spring and summer.

- **Late October to Early November:** Once the summer crowds have dispersed and before the major religious celebrations of All Saints' Day (November 1st) and the Christmas season begin, late October and early November offer a relatively calm period for visiting. This is also a pleasant time of year in terms of weather.

- **Mid-November to Early December:** With the exception of special events, this period tends to be quieter, as most visitors wait until the holiday season to travel. It's also a good time to visit as Rome gears up for Christmas without the full influx of holiday travelers.

- **Early September (Before Major Fall Events):** The early part of September, after the summer holidays but before the Feast of Saints Peter and Paul and other major autumn festivals, can offer a quieter window for visiting the city.

Why These Weeks Are Ideal:

These weeks fall between major religious holidays, avoiding the peak crowds of Christmas, Easter, and summer. While there will still be Jubilee pilgrims, the overall volume of visitors will be lower, making it easier to navigate Rome's major sites and pilgrimage routes. These periods also offer the chance to enjoy a more peaceful experience at Rome's basilicas, museums, and historical landmarks without long lines or overcrowding.

By planning your visit during these off-peak weeks, you'll still be able to participate in Jubilee events while avoiding the largest crowds, giving you more time and space to reflect and explore the city's treasures.

Practical Information and Tips

- **Transportation:** Rome's public transportation system will be enhanced to accommodate the influx of visitors, but expect delays and crowded conditions. The Metro A line, which runs near key pilgrimage sites such as the Vatican and St. John Lateran, will be essential for navigating the city efficiently. It's advisable to book accommodation near transportation hubs to minimize travel time.

- **Accommodation:** Hotels, hostels, and religious guest houses in Rome are expected to be fully booked months in advance, especially during peak weeks. Early reservations are highly recommended. Consider staying in nearby areas such as Trastevere, Prati, or Aventino for easier access to major sites without the overwhelming crowds.

- **Security:** Enhanced security measures will be in place, especially around Vatican City and major pilgrimage sites. It's advisable to arrive early for events, as security checks may take time. Be vigilant about your belongings in crowded areas to avoid petty theft, which can be common during large gatherings.

- **Food and Rest:** Plan breaks between visiting sites to avoid exhaustion, especially during the summer months when Rome can get very hot. Many cafes and trattorias will offer special menus catering to pilgrims. Make reservations for lunch and dinner through google maps, this saves you time and ensures no one gets hangry.

Conclusion: Why the Jubilee Year Matters

The Jubilee Year offers more than a religious experience—it is an opportunity to connect with centuries of tradition, history, and faith. Whether you are a pilgrim seeking indulgence, a traveler curious about the Church's most significant celebrations, or someone drawn to the cultural and historical depth of the event, the Jubilee Year in Rome will be an unforgettable experience. Rome in 2025 will serve as the heart of this remarkable tradition, offering visitors a chance to walk through history and faith, tracing the footsteps of millions of pilgrims who have sought grace and renewal through this sacred ritual.

CHAPTER FIVE

Opening of the Holy Doors

A Sacred Ritual for the Jubilee Year 2025

The Jubilee Year is traditionally inaugurated by the opening of the Holy Doors (Porta Santa) of the four papal basilicas in Rome. These doors, sealed during ordinary years, are only opened during a Jubilee to symbolize the extraordinary path of mercy and forgiveness that the faithful are invited to walk through. The act of passing through the Holy Doors represents the soul's journey toward salvation.

- **Christmas Eve, 2024:** The Jubilee celebrations officially begin with the opening of the Holy Door at St. Peter's Basilica, a tradition dating back to 1500 during the papacy of Alexander VI. This deeply symbolic act holds great significance in the Catholic Church and marks the start of the Holy Year.

- **29 December, 2024:** Pope Francis will open the Holy Door of the Archbasilica of St. John Lateran, the Cathedral of Rome. On this same day, every Cathedral and co-Cathedral around the world will celebrate Mass, led by the local Bishop, to inaugurate the Jubilee in their regions.

- **1 January, 2025**: The Pope will open the Holy Door of the Basilica of St. Mary Major during the Solemnity of Mary, the Mother of God, one of the most important feasts in the Catholic calendar.

- **5 January, 2025 (Vigil of Epiphany):** The Holy Door of the Basilica of St. Paul Outside the Walls will be opened, concluding the series of Holy Door openings for the major pilgrimage sites in Rome.

Pope Francis has called for active participation throughout this Holy Year, writing that "every effort should be made to enable the People of God to participate fully in its proclamation of hope in God's grace and in the signs that attest to their efficacy." This emphasizes the universal call to grace and renewal, inviting Catholics from around the world to take part in this extraordinary period of reflection and spiritual growth.

Throughout the Jubilee Year, these doors will be open to welcome pilgrims worldwide, granting them plenary indulgences. More detail about these four Papal Basilicas in the Giro of the Sette Chiese Chapter.

Besides the four papal basilicas, Pope Francis has also expressed his desire to open a Holy Door in prison, offering a powerful symbol of mercy and inclusion for inmates, marking the Jubilee as a time of forgiveness and compassion.

Indulgences and Spiritual Acts

A key feature of the Jubilee, rooted in the tradition since its inception in 1300, is the granting of plenary indulgences. These indulgences express God's boundless forgiveness, obtainable through acts of penance, charity, and hope. Pilgrims are encouraged to take part in the sacrament of penance, receive the Eucharist, and pray for the Holy Father's intentions.

Special Events and Celebrations

There will be a wide range of religious, cultural, and social events across Rome and the Vatican. From solemn masses in St. Peter's Square to exhibitions, concerts, and spiritual gatherings, the city will be alive with devotion and celebration, welcoming pilgrims from around the globe. Particular attention will be given to charitable acts and the spiritual renewal of the faithful, underscoring the Jubilee's theme of "Pilgrims of Hope."

The Jubilee will draw to a close on 28 December 2025 in churches across the world, with the Holy Doors of St. John Lateran, St. Mary Major, and St. Paul Outside the Walls closing on the same date. Finally, the Jubilee Year will formally conclude in Rome on the Solemnity of Epiphany, 6 January 2026, bringing an end to this significant period of celebration and grace for the global Catholic community.

CHAPTER SIX

Booking Accommodation in Rome

Choosing the Best Area for Your Visit

When booking accommodation in Rome, it's important to find a location that provides easy access to the city's major landmarks while also offering a pleasant neighborhood atmosphere. Staying in the historic center is ideal for those looking to immerse themselves in the city's vibrant past and culture while minimizing travel time between attractions.

Focus your search on these recommended neighborhoods:

*For more detailed Accommodation information, see **Accommodation Detail Chapter** toward the end of the book.

Centro Storico (Historical Center)

The Centro Storico is the heart of Rome, a lively, picturesque district brimming with iconic landmarks, charming streets, and layers of historical treasures. Staying here allows you to immerse yourself in Rome's atmosphere, with famous attractions like the Pantheon, Piazza Navona, and Campo de' Fiori just a short stroll away.

This area is ideal for travelers who want to experience Rome's vibrant daily life, surrounded by bustling cafés, stylish boutiques, and cozy trattorias. Accommodations range from luxurious, high-end hotels with breathtaking rooftop terraces to intimate boutique hotels and guest houses, each offering a unique perspective on Roman culture. With its cobblestone alleys and historical charm, the Centro Storico lets you feel the timeless energy of the Eternal City right at your doorstep.

- Pros: Central location, walkable to major sites, vibrant atmosphere with restaurants, shops, and bars.

- Cons: Higher prices because of its popularity with tourists.

Trastevere

Located just across the Tiber River, Trastevere is a picturesque, bohemian neighborhood renowned for its cobbled streets, vibrant nightlife, and charming atmosphere. While slightly removed from the main tourist crowds, it's still very accessible to major sites like the Vatican and the Colosseum, and provides a more authentic Roman experience. Trastevere is also recognized for its array of restaurants, offering delicious Roman cuisine.

- Pros: Authentic Roman vibe, great food, lively atmosphere, still close to major attractions.

- Cons: Can be busy and noisy at night because of the nightlife.

Monti

Monti is one of Rome's oldest neighborhoods, near the Colosseum and the Roman Forum. It has a mix of trendy boutiques, quaint cafes, and cozy trattorias. Monti offers a quieter, more local feel, while still being close to Rome's historical sites. This area is perfect for travelers looking to enjoy a neighborhood experience while staying in proximity to major attractions.

- Pros: Close to major sites, local charm, trendy and artsy.

- Cons: Fewer large hotels, mostly smaller boutique options.

Vatican / Prati

For those interested in visiting St. Peter's Basilica and the Vatican Museums, the Prati neighborhood is ideal. It's located just north of the Vatican and offers a more residential feel. Prati is famous for its wide, elegant streets and excellent shopping opportunities.

- Pros: Quiet and elegant, close to the Vatican, good for shopping.

- Cons: Further from the ancient Roman sites like the Colosseum and Roman Forum.

Spanish Steps / Piazza di Spagna

Staying near the Spanish Steps places you in one of Rome's most iconic and upscale areas. This neighborhood is home to luxury shopping streets like

Via Condotti and is close to both the Trevi Fountain and Villa Borghese. Hotels in this area range from five-star properties to boutique guesthouses.

- Pros: Upscale, luxury shopping, central to many attractions.

- Cons: Higher accommodation prices and can be crowded with tourists.

Termini Station Area

For budget-conscious travelers, the area around Termini Station offers a wide range of affordable hotels, hostels, and guesthouses. While the area isn't as charming as the Centro Storico, it's well-connected via Rome's public transport system and offers easy access to both the metro and train lines, including transport to and from Rome's airports.

- Pros: Budget-friendly, excellent transport connections.

- Cons: Less charming, can feel a bit more hectic and less safe at night.

Campo de' Fiori / Piazza Navona (my preferred location)

These neighborhoods are at the heart of historic Rome, with picturesque piazzas and vibrant street life. Campo de' Fiori is known for its daily market, while Piazza Navona is one of the city's most beautiful squares. Staying here places you within walking distance of key attractions like the Pantheon, Trevi Fountain, and Capitoline Hill.

- Pros: Central, historic, lively squares, walkable to all major sites.

- Cons: Crowded and can be noisy because of the street markets and restaurants.

Types of Accommodation in Rome

*See Accommodation Detail Chapter for more information.

Hotels: Ranging from luxury five-star properties to small boutique hotels, Rome offers a wide selection of hotel options in every price range.

Guest houses & B&Bs: A great option for travelers looking for a more personalized experience, often in charming historical buildings.

Vacation Rentals: Perfect for families or larger groups, vacation rentals give you more space and a kitchen.

Booking Tips

Book Early: Accommodation in Rome will fill up quickly, so it's best to book several months in advance.

Stay Central: Rome is best experienced on foot, and staying in or near the city center ensures you are never far from the action.

Consider Accessibility: If you have mobility concerns, look for accommodations close to metro stations or with good transportation links.

By focusing your accommodation search in one of these neighborhoods, you'll be perfectly positioned to explore Rome's rich history, culture, and religious significance, all while enjoying the comfort and convenience of being close to the city's most iconic landmarks.

CHAPTER SEVEN

The Papal Bull

The Central Message: Hope in God's Mercy

O n May 9, 2024, Pope Francis issued the papal bull Spes Non Confundit ("Hope Does Not Disappoint"), officially proclaiming the Jubilee Year 2025. Rooted in the Apostle Paul's words to the Christian community of Rome, this document emphasizes hope as the central theme and calls on pilgrims worldwide to embark on a journey of faith, forgiveness, and renewal.

The Central Message: Hope in God's Mercy

The phrase "Hope does not disappoint" (Romans 5:5) captures the essence of the Jubilee, reminding Christians that their hope is anchored in God's unfailing love. Pope Francis invites all pilgrims, whether they travel to Rome or celebrate in their local churches, to experience this Holy Year as a profound, personal encounter with Jesus Christ—the door to salvation.

This Jubilee will focus on rekindling hope in a world often marred by uncertainty, fear, and conflict. Pope Francis addresses the modern challenges of doubt, anxiety, and impatience, urging Christians to cultivate the virtue of patience—closely tied to hope—as an antidote to the "frenetic haste" of today's world.

Saint John Paul II

A quarter of a century before the 2025 Jubilee, St. John Paul II wrote in Incarnationis Mysterium, his bull of indiction for the Great Jubilee of 2000, about the powerful symbolism of the Holy Door. He explained that it "evokes the passage from sin to grace which every Christian is called to accomplish."

In doing so, St. John Paul II drew on Jesus' own words from Scripture: "I am the door" (John 10:7), making it clear that Christ alone is the gateway to eternal salvation. "There is only one way that opens wide the entrance into the life of communion with God: this is Jesus, the one and absolute way to salvation." The Holy Door thus becomes not just a symbol, but a tangible invitation to all believers, echoing the words of the Psalmist: "This is the door of the Lord where the just may enter" (Psalm 118:20). [1]

John Paul II further reflected on the responsibility of every believer to pass through the Holy Door. To do so, he wrote, is not a mere physical act but a profound spiritual decision, acknowledging Christ as Lord. He likened this passage to a moment of grace-filled choice: "To pass through that door means to confess that Jesus Christ is Lord; it is to strengthen faith in him in order to live the new life which he has given us." It is a symbolic gesture

---

1. *Cited from* "5 Holy Doors: What Every Catholic Should Know Ahead of Jubilee 2025," *National Catholic Register*, accessed October 26, 2024, https://www.ncregister.com/news/5-holy-doors-what-every-catholic-should-know-ahead-of-jubilee-2025 .

of leaving behind the old life of sin and entering into a renewed life of grace and communion with God, as outlined in the parable of the treasure hidden in the field (Matthew 13:44-46).

CHAPTER EIGHT

Your Key to the Jubilee Year 2025

Carta del Pellegrino

To enhance the experience for pilgrims, the Vatican has introduced the Carta del Pellegrino (Pilgrim's Card). This free digital card is essential for participating in the events of the Jubilee and organizing your pilgrimage to the Holy Door. This personalized digital card not only streamlines access to major events but also offers practical benefits for pilgrims.

What Is the Carta del Pellegrino?

The Carta del Pellegrino (pilgrims card) is a digital, nominal card that allows pilgrims to:

- Register for events, including the pilgrimage to the Holy Door of St. Peter's Basilica.

- Organize their pilgrimage with the ability to manage bookings for specific days, times, and events.

- Access discounts on transport, accommodation, restaurants, mobility services, and cultural events throughout Rome.

The card ensures an organized and efficient flow of pilgrims at high-demand events, helping to prevent overcrowding and facilitating a smooth pilgrimage experience.

To acquire the Carta del Pellegrino, pilgrims must register through the official Jubilee portal:

- Visit register.iubilaeum2025.va or use the official Jubilee app.

- After entering your details, you will receive a personalized QR code and an account on the app, which will serve as your digital identification throughout the events.

Once you have obtained your Carta del Pellegrino, you can sign up for the pilgrimage to the Holy Door of St. Peter's and other key Jubilee events through the website or app. This registration system helps manage the large number of pilgrims attending and ensures an orderly process for accessing significant religious sites and events.

You can:

- You can register individually or as a group.

- Indicate any disabilities or special requirements.

- Manage, modify, or cancel your bookings.

The card is an essential tool to make your Jubilee pilgrimage more convenient, offering both organizational support and exclusive benefits, ensuring that your spiritual journey during the Holy Year is as smooth and fulfilling as possible.

CHAPTER NINE

Centro Pellegrini

The Pilgrim's Information Point for all Things Jubolee

F or pilgrims, the Centro Pellegrini (Pilgrim Information Point) serves as a key resource for essential information and support. At Via della Conciliazione, 7 (street addresses in Italy end with the number), just steps from St. Peter's Basilica, this center is the go-to place for pilgrims and tourists seeking guidance on how to participate in the Holy Year events.

Services and Resources

The Centro Pellegrini is open daily from 10:00 AM to 5:00 PM and offers a wide range of services and information to ensure a meaningful and smooth pilgrimage experience. These include:

Information on Events

- **Pilgrimage to the Holy Door**: Learn how to participate in the ceremonial pilgrimage to the Holy Door of St. Peter's Basilica, a central tradition of the Jubilee Year.

- **Major Events and Celebrations**: Stay updated on papal audiences, liturgical celebrations, and special events throughout the Holy Year.

Material Distribution

The center provides free resources and materials to help pilgrims navigate Rome and make the most of their visit:

- **Brochures and Maps**: Detailed guides of pilgrimage routes and historic itineraries.

- **Pilgrimage of the Seven Churches**: A historic route that includes visits to Rome's most significant basilicas, such as St. John Lateran, St. Mary Major, and St. Paul Outside the Walls.

- **Women Doctors and Patrons of Europe**: An itinerary celebrating the contributions of influential female saints like St. Teresa of Ávila and St. Catherine of Siena.

Assistance Services

- **Pilgrim Registration**: Assistance with registering for Jubilee events and obtaining the Pilgrim's Certificate, a keepsake recognizing participation in the Holy Year.

- **Language Support**: Multilingual staff are available to assist visitors in a variety of languages, including English, Italian, Spanish, and French.

- **Accessibility Information**: Resources and advice for pilgrims with mobility challenges, ensuring that everyone can participate in Jubilee activities.

Additional Features

- **Prayer and Reflection Spaces**: The Centro Pellegrini also offers designated quiet spaces for prayer, reflection, and spiritual preparation before embarking on pilgrimage activities.

- **Gift Shop**: A small shop within the center provides souvenirs, prayer cards, and religious items, including rosaries blessed by the Pope.

- **Cultural Exhibitions**: The center occasionally hosts exhibitions and displays related to the history of the Jubilee Year and pilgrimage traditions.

Tips for Visiting

- **Arrive Early**: Lines can form during peak times, especially on weekends or when major events are scheduled.

- **Bring Identification**: If you plan to register for events or volunteer opportunities, having a passport or ID on hand is helpful.

- **Ask Questions**: The staff is well-informed and can provide valuable insider tips to enhance your experience.

Whether you are a first-time visitor or a seasoned pilgrim, the Centro Pellegrini is a welcoming and invaluable resource to guide you through your spiritual journey in Rome.

CHAPTER TEN

Jubilees Through the Centuries

Walking the Sacred Path

W hen I first started writing this book and began speaking with locals in Rome, I found myself increasingly fascinated by a single question: What was Rome like during other Jubilee celebrations throughout history? This curiosity sparked an exploration into the experiences of pilgrims over the centuries, journeying to the Eternal City in search of spiritual renewal, indulgences, and divine grace. In these chapters, I'll take you back in time, allowing you to walk in the footsteps of these past pilgrims, experiencing the challenges, sights, and emotions they encountered.

As we journey through different Jubilee years of 1300, 1500 and 1650, you'll follow the paths of pilgrims from medieval times through the Renaissance and Baroque eras. You'll feel their anticipation as they approach Rome for the first time, face the hardships of the long journey, and marvel at the transformations of the city and its sacred spaces over the centuries. From navigating ancient streets to witnessing the development of St. Peter's Basilica, this section will immerse you in the deep historical and profound spiritual significance of Rome's Jubilees, showing how this holy tradition has developed while maintaining its timeless essence.

The First Jubilee -The Year 1300

Upon reaching the Eternal City in the year 1300, while you may be tired and road-weary from your journey, you are still filled with the thrill of entering Rome. This pilgrimage to Rome for the first-ever Jubilee is not just a spiritual journey but a once-in-a-lifetime opportunity for the full remission of sins. The city you're about to enter is a medieval marvel, still bearing the scars of recent conflicts between the Papal States and the Holy Roman Empire, but pulsing with religious fervor.

The Journey to Rome

Your journey to Rome has been arduous and fraught with danger. If you're coming from distant lands like Spain or Austria, you've been on the road for two to three months, covering about 20-30 kilometers per day. You've faced numerous challenges:

- Safety: You've traveled in groups for protection against bandits and wild animals that prowl the roads.

- Lodging: You've relied on a network of hostels, monasteries, and hospitals along popular pilgrimage routes, often sleeping on hard floors.

- Food: Your diet has comprised dried meats, hard cheeses, and bread that could last for days. You've foraged for berries and nuts and hunted small game. Fasting was part of a pilgrim's life.

- Water: You've collected water from streams and wells, and you're always wary of contamination that could bring illness.

- Clothing: You wear a long robe and a wide-brimmed hat for protection from the sun. Your pilgrim's staff has served as both support and defense.

- Identification: You wear a pilgrim's badge, identifying you as a traveler seeking spiritual renewal, sometimes offering protection and eliciting charity from locals.

First Glimpse of Rome

As Rome appears, you're captivated by the sight of the ancient Aurelian Walls, erected in the 3rd century AD. The city is encircled by massive fortifications, showcasing Rome's turbulent history. Unlike in future centuries, St. Peter's Basilica doesn't dominate the skyline - the current St. Peter's won't be built for another 200 years. Instead, you see the outline of the old Constantinian basilica.

The city within the walls is a dense maze of medieval streets and ancient ruins. Rome in 1300 is recovering from years of conflict between noble families, and many ancient monuments lie in disrepair. Yet, the city is alive with fresh energy as pilgrims from all over Christendom converge for this unprecedented event.

Entering the Eternal City in 1300

Your entry into Rome depends on your direction of approach:

From the North: Porta del Popolo (Porta Flaminia)

You enter through the Porta del Popolo, then known as Porta Flaminia. This gate, rebuilt in the 6th century by Belisarius, stands as a formidable entrance to the city. As you pass through, you're struck by the contrast between the countryside you've left behind and the bustling urban landscape before you.

The church of Santa Maria del Popolo, while present, is not yet the grand Renaissance structure it will become. In 1300, it was a much simpler church, originally built in 1099 to exorcise the ghost of Nero, believed to haunt the area. Pilgrims often stop here to give thanks for their safe arrival and to seek blessings for their time in Rome.

The Piazza del Popolo doesn't exist as we know it today. Instead, you find yourself in a less formal open area, crowded with pilgrims, merchants, and locals. No central obelisk or fountain exists yet. The space is more utilitarian, serving as a gathering point and market area.

Here, three streets converge to create the "trident" that will define this area. The central street, the Via Lata (future Via del Corso), is the principal route into the heart of Rome. It's crowded with pilgrims, many looking as bewildered as you feel.

Find your way to St. Peter's by:

- Asking fellow pilgrims or locals for directions. Many Romans are used to guiding visitors.

- Following the crowd, as many are heading to the same destination.

- Looking for clergy or members of religious orders who often guide pilgrims.

- Seeking out one of the many informal "guides" offering their services (though beware of scams).

The route to St. Peter's in 1300 is not straightforward, as the medieval city of Rome is a maze of narrow, winding streets. To reach the Vatican area, you will cross the Ponte Elio, as it was known at the time, a key bridge over the Tiber River. Originally built in 134 AD by Emperor Hadrian to connect the city to his mausoleum (now Castel Sant'Angelo), this bridge has long been a vital passageway for pilgrims.

By the time of the Jubilee in 1300, the Ponte Elio is already an essential route for those making their way to St. Peter's Basilica.

From the South: Porta San Paolo (Porta Ostiense)

Entering through this gate, you're immediately struck by the nearby Pyramid of Cestius, an ancient Roman tomb incorporated into the Aurelian Walls. The area is less crowded than the northern entrance, but still bustling with activity.

You see the massive Basilica of Saint Paul Outside the Walls in the distance, a major pilgrimage site. Many pilgrims stop here before continuing to the city center and St. Peter's.

To reach St. Peter's from here, you'd need to navigate through the city, perhaps following the Tiber northward. The journey takes you through the heart of medieval Rome, past ancient ruins and crowded markets.

From the East: Porta Maggiore

This impressive double-arched gate, built into an ancient Roman aqueduct, welcomes you with its monumental presence. The area around the gate is less developed, with vineyards and orchards visible just inside the walls.

The path to St. Peter's is quite long and winding. You'd likely make your way towards the Lateran area first, where you might stop at the Basilica of

St. John Lateran, the cathedral of Rome, before continuing westward to the Vatican.

From the West: Porta Septimiana or Porta Aurelia

If you're already coming from the Vatican area, you might enter the city proper through one of these gates. The Porta Septimiana leads you into the Trastevere neighborhood, a bustling area with a character distinct from the rest of Rome.

From either of these gates, you're relatively close to St. Peter's, but you still need to navigate the crowded streets of medieval Rome to reach other important sites.

Navigation in Medieval Rome in 1300

Regardless of your entry point, finding your way to St. Peter's and other sites in 1300 Rome is challenging. There are no street signs or official maps to guide you, and the streets are narrow and winding, with names often changing multiple times. Many of the landmarks familiar to modern visitors don't exist yet, adding to the confusion. The city is crowded with other pilgrims, many of whom are just as lost as you are, making navigation through the bustling medieval streets a daunting task.

A City of Faith

Rome in 1300 is the unquestioned center of Western Christendom, and as you make your way through its crowded streets, you are immediately struck by the omnipresence of the Church. Everywhere you turn, priests, monks, and friars are visible, particularly from the mendicant orders like the Franciscans and Dominicans, which had been founded less than a century earlier. The city is dotted with hundreds of churches, ranging from tiny chapels to grand basilicas, many of which are ancient structures repurposed from Roman temples or built during the early Christian era.

Surrounding you are fellow pilgrims from all walks of life—nobles and peasants, young and old—united in their quest for spiritual renewal. The sense of devotion is palpable, and as you navigate through the city, you hear whispers about the countless relics housed in Rome's churches. Pilgrims speak with awe of sacred objects like the Veil of Veronica, said to display Christ's face at Old St. Peter's Basilica, adding to the spiritual intensity of the journey.

Approaching Saint Peter's Basilica

As you make your way towards the basilica, you navigate through the area known as the Borgo. Unlike in later centuries, this area is not yet fully developed. The Leonine Walls, built in the 9th century to protect the Vatican area, are still clearly visible.

The approach to St. Peter's is not the grand avenue it will become in later centuries. Instead, you wind through narrow, irregular streets, catching glimpses of the basilica as you go. The anticipation builds with each turn.

The Original Basilica di San Pietro

You emerge into the square before the original basilica. The building before you is not the grand Renaissance structure of later centuries but the ancient church built by Constantine in the 4th century. Its façade is adorned with glittering mosaics, and a grand staircase leads up to the entrance.

The square is packed with pilgrims. Some are entering the church, others are exiting with looks of awe on their faces, and many are simply sitting or kneeling in prayer. The atmosphere is one of intense spiritual fervor.

Inside the Basilica

As you enter the basilica, you're struck by its size and splendor. The nave stretches out before you, lined with columns taken from ancient Roman buildings. The walls are covered with frescoes and mosaics depicting biblical scenes and saints.

In the year 1300, the Basilica di San Pietro was a monumental structure filled with art and spiritual grandeur, though it differed from the basilica we know today. The original basilica, built under Emperor Constantine in the 4th century, had stood for nearly a millennium by the time of the first Jubilee, making it an important religious and architectural site. Its cruciform shape was vast for its time, with a long nave that stretched over 100 meters and could accommodate thousands of pilgrims.

Shape and Size of St. Peter's Basilica

The basilica was laid out in the shape of a cross, with a long nave, a transept crossing the nave, and a semicircular apse at the end. Five aisles made up the structure, the central nave being the widest and tallest. The length of the basilica stretched approximately 118 meters (around 387 feet), and the nave's width was about 64 meters (210 feet).

Many of the columns that lined the nave were spolia, taken from ancient Roman temples and repurposed for the church. These columns gave the church a mix of classical and early Christian styles.

Art Inside

By 1300, the basilica was adorned with a variety of artworks, mostly frescoes and mosaics, created by earlier medieval artists. Several generations of artists have left their mark:

- Frescoes and mosaics: The interior walls were covered in biblical scenes, including depictions of Christ, the Virgin Mary, the Apostles, and saints. These mosaics were a hallmark of early

Christian and Byzantine-inspired art, made with rich colors, gold backgrounds, and stylized figures.

- Artists: While specific artists from earlier centuries were anonymous or unknown, some known names associated with the decoration of St. Peter's include:

- Pietro Cavallini: An influential Roman artist working in the late 13th century, Cavallini created beautiful frescoes and mosaics, some of which might have adorned the basilica's walls. He was known for his ability to bring realism and emotion into religious art, bridging the Romanesque and Gothic styles.

- Mosaicists from the Byzantine tradition: Much of the mosaic work in Old St. Peter's reflected the influence of Byzantine art, with earlier mosaicists creating some of the vibrant depictions of saints and religious narratives in the apse and along the walls.

The Tomb of the Saint

At the heart of the basilica was the tomb of St. Peter beneath the high altar. This was the spiritual centerpiece of the basilica and the ultimate destination for pilgrims. The tomb, which houses the remains of the Apostle Peter, was adorned with precious materials and surrounded by rich decoration. In 1300, pilgrims would often crowd the area, as touching or praying near the tomb was believed to bring blessings and indulgences.

Despite the ancient nature of the original Basilica San Pietro by this time, the basilica's size and the reverence surrounding it left pilgrims in awe, making their journey to this sacred space the pinnacle of their spiritual experience.

Rome Beyond St. Peter's

While St. Peter's is the focus of your pilgrimage, Rome in 1300 offers a wealth of other sacred sites and ancient wonders. As a pilgrim, you're drawn to visit as many holy places as possible, each offering its spiritual significance and the promise of indulgences.

Major Pilgrimage Churches in 1300

Basilica di San Giovanni in Laterano: The cathedral of Rome and the seat of the Pope, the Lateran Basilica and palace complex is a center of spiritual and political power. It houses important relics, including what are believed to be the heads of Saints Peter and Paul.

Basilica di Santa Maria Maggiore: This ancient basilica, dedicated to the Virgin Mary, draws many pilgrims with its beautiful mosaics and relics. It's said to contain wood from Christ's manger.

Basilica di San Paolo Fuori le Mura (St. Paul Outside the Walls): This basilica, built over the tomb of St. Paul, is a crucial stop for pilgrims. Despite being outside the city walls, many people journey to pray at the apostle's resting place.

Basilica di San Lorenzo Fuori le Mura (St. Lawrence Outside the Walls): Another important extramural church, it houses the tomb of St. Lawrence and attracts many pilgrims.

Early Christian Churches

Chiesa di Santa Pudenziana: Near Santa Maria Maggiore, this church is believed to be one of the oldest in Rome. Today, the church's most famous feature, the 5th-century apse mosaic, remains unchanged. The mosaic depicts Christ enthroned among the Apostles, with a backdrop of Jerusalem. This mosaic, one of Rome's oldest Christian artworks, would have been a major attraction for pilgrims. The art reflects an early Christian understanding of Christ's kingship and the Church's authority.

Chiesa di Santa Prassede: Close to Santa Maria Maggiore, this church houses a segment of the alleged pillar upon which Christ was flogged. The church's ninth century mosaics, commissioned by Pope Paschal I, would have left visitors in awe. The church's highlight mosaics include the stunning apse mosaic of Christ, the Apostles, and saints, as well as the well-preserved mosaic work in the Chapel of Saint Zeno.

Ancient mosaics in the Chiesa di Santa Prassede

Pilgrims in 1300 would have marveled at the colorful depictions of Christian saints, angels, and biblical scenes, seeing in them a reflection of the heavenly world. The gold background of these mosaics would have glimmered in the dim candlelight, creating an atmosphere of spiritual transcendence.

Chiesa di Santi Quattro Coronati: This fortified church complex on the Caelian Hill, though less grand than some, attracts pilgrims with its air of antiquity and sanctity.

Ancient Roman Sites Converted to Churches by 1300

The Pantheon: This ancient Roman temple, now converted into the church of Santa Maria ad Martyres, astounds visitors with its massive dome and oculus. It's a powerful symbol of the triumph of Christianity over paganism. The Pantheon was officially converted into a Christian church in the year 609 AD. This transformation occurred under the reign of the Byzantine Emperor Phocas, who gifted the building to Pope Boniface IV. On May 13, 609, the Pantheon was consecrated as the church of Santa Maria ad Martyres (Saint Mary and the Martyrs).

San Clemente: This multi-layered church offers pilgrims a journey through time, with its 12th-century basilica built over a 4th-century church, which stands above a 1st-century Roman house and a Mithraic temple. San Clemente refers to Pope Clement I, one of the earliest bishops of Rome and traditionally considered the third pope after Saint Peter. He is regarded as a martyr and a significant figure in early Christianity. By the time of the first Jubilee in 1300, the Basilica of San Clemente was an essential pilgrimage site because of its rich history, architectural complexity, and spiritual significance. The church represented the layered history of Christianity in Rome, with its multi-layered construction offering visitors a literal journey through time.

Other Significant Sites

The Roman Forum: While many ancient structures lie in ruins, this area serves as a reminder of Rome's imperial past. Some ancient temples here have been converted into churches.

Scala Santa: The Scala Santa comprises 28 white marble steps and is believed by tradition to be the staircase that Jesus ascended during His trial before Pontius Pilate in Jerusalem. Based on Christian tradition, the stairs were brought to Rome by St. Helena, the mother of Emperor Constantine, in the 4th century. These "Holy Stairs," believed to be from

Pilate's palace in Jerusalem, are a popular site for penitential climbing on one's knees.

By the time of the first event of 1300, the Scala Santa was already regarded as one of the most sacred relics in Christendom, attracting pilgrims from all over Europe. The traditions associated with it involved:

- Ascension on Knees: Pilgrims would ascend the Scala Santa on their knees, pausing at each step to pray. In remembrance of Christ's Passion, climbing the stairs symbolizes penitence and devotion.

- Indulgences: The Scala Santa was closely tied to the granting of indulgences. During 1300, Pope Boniface VIII offered a plenary indulgence (the full remission of sins) to pilgrims who explored the basilicas of St. Peter and St. Paul, and the Scala Santa became part of the pilgrimage circuit. Climbing the stairs on one's knees was believed to earn special graces and remission of sins.

- Devotion to the Passion of Christ: The Scala Santa represented a physical connection to Christ's Passion, and pilgrims who ascended it engaged in deep contemplation of His suffering. This practice reinforced the spiritual significance of their pilgrimage to Rome when the city was filled with a sense of renewal and spiritual fervor.

Pilgrims' Accommodations

Lodging in Rome during the Jubilee is a significant challenge because of the massive influx of pilgrims. Options include:

- Hospices: Many religious orders operate hospices for pilgrims. These offer basic accommodation, often just a place to sleep on the floor and perhaps a simple meal.

- Monasteries and Convents: Some open their doors to pilgrims, offering sparse but clean lodging.

- Pilgrims' Hostels: Established along major pilgrimage routes and near important churches, these provide basic shelter.

- Private Homes: Some Romans rent out space in their homes to pilgrims, though this can be expensive.

- Campgrounds: In and around the city, impromptu campgrounds spring up to accommodate the overflow of pilgrims.

- National Hospices: Some nations or regions have established hospices in Rome for their pilgrims. For example, the Schola Francorum near St. Peter's serves French pilgrims.

Many pilgrims, especially the poor, sleep in church porticos, on the steps of public buildings, or wherever they can find space.

The challenge of finding accommodation adds to the penitential nature of the pilgrimage. Despite the hardships, the shared experience of visiting these holy sites and navigating the crowded, chaotic city deepens the sense of spiritual journey and community among pilgrims.

Length of Stay

The length of stay for pilgrims depended on several factors, including their origin and financial means. Many pilgrims from distant lands stayed for weeks, possibly months, to justify their long journey. Wealthy attendees may choose to prolong their stay to fully engage in the event's spiritual advantages. Poorer pilgrims may have only stayed as long as needed to visit the required holy sites, often being supported by alms from the Roman population or Church institutions.

There is historical evidence that the city was overwhelmed by the sheer number of pilgrims, many of whom required shelter and food, leading to a thriving system of hostels and charitable institutions dedicated to helping travelers.

1300 Jubilee Reflection

As your pilgrimage ends, you're overwhelmed by the experience. You've traveled countless miles, faced many hardships, and now stand within the epicenter of Christendom. You've prayed at the tombs of apostles, witnessed the power and glory of the Church, and joined with fellow pilgrims in a profound act of faith.

The first celebration of 1300 has been a transformative experience, not just for individuals but for the entire Christian world. As you prepare for your journey home, you carry with you not just the promise of spiritual renewal, but memories that will last a lifetime. Those who took part in a historic moment, the beginning of a tradition that will shape Christian pilgrimage for centuries to come.

A Pilgrim's Journey to Rome: The Jubilee of 1500

As you approach the Eternal City at the dawn of a new century, your heart fills with excitement. This pilgrimage for the Jubilee of 1500 promises not just spiritual renewal but a rich experience of Renaissance Rome, a city on the cusp of transformation under the reign of Pope Alexander VI.

First Glimpse of Rome

Upon first sight of Rome, the city's iconic Aurelian Walls stretch before you, symbolizing its ancient grandeur. Beyond them, you catch glimpses of the vibrant Renaissance architecture, with ongoing construction shaping the skyline. The Vatican area, particularly the site of St. Peter's Basilica, is your ultimate destination, though the basilica itself remains a medieval structure awaiting future reconstruction.

Unlike future Jubilees, the Vatican is not yet a separate entity; it is still an integral part of the larger Papal States. Within the Leonine Walls, there is a bustling crowd of pilgrims, clergy, and merchants. In the Borgo district, the medieval streets are brimming with shops, houses, and hospices that are dedicated to supporting the influx of visitors.

Entering the Eternal City in 1500

Depending on your place of origin, the paths into the city will vary.

From Spain (West): Entering through the ancient Porta del Popolo. The sight of Renaissance-era buildings intermixed with medieval structures fills you with awe.

From Europe (North): Passing through the piazza where the Spanish Embassy stands, you encounter Spanish pilgrims gathered under the warm Roman sun, resting before their journey continues. By this time, the Spanish monarchs Ferdinand and Isabella had established permanent diplomatic representation at the papal court. Spain maintained one of the most important embassies in Rome during this period, as the Catholic Monarchs were key allies of the papacy.

Under Alexander VI (Rodrigo Borgia, Pope from 1492-1503), Spain's influence in Rome was particularly strong, not least because Alexander VI himself was Spanish.

From the South: As you approach St. John Lateran, the Mother Church of Rome, you feel the spiritual energy of pilgrims preparing for confession before entering the city proper. The Lateran Basilica is at the heart of early festivities.

From the East: Entering through the Porta Maggiore, your path takes you past the remnants of ancient Roman baths and aqueducts, which stand as silent witnesses to the city's imperial past.

Once inside, you find that every fountain and public square is alive, with pilgrims filling their flasks and washing the dust of their journey. The city, shaped by centuries of Christian devotion, embraces you with open arms.

Again A City of Faith

In 1500, religious orders dominated the streets of Rome: monks, nuns, and clergy of every kind crowded the city. You see Dominicans, Franciscans, and Benedictines offering guidance and aid to pilgrims. The newly formed Jesuit order has not yet risen to prominence, leaving older religious communities to serve the multitudes.

Behind the walls of convents, cloistered nuns like the Poor Clares and Carmelites maintain a constant prayer vigil. The hospitality offered by these religious figures—whether providing food, lodging, or spiritual direction—gives you a sense of deep Christian charity.

Approaching St. Peter's Basilica in 1500

Navigating the dense medieval streets of the Borgo, you reach St. Peter's Basilica, still the old basilica that had stood for centuries. In the Jubilee Year of 1500, St. Peter's Basilica was still the ancient basilica built by Emperor Constantine in the 4th century. Over 1,100 years had passed, making the structure one of Christendom's most revered pilgrimage sites. Pilgrims flocked to it during the Jubilee to pray at the tomb of St. Peter and seek the indulgences offered by the Church.

However, the basilica was showing signs of age, with portions of the structure deteriorating because of the passage of time and past conflicts. The idea of rebuilding St. Peter's was already circulating, but the grand project for the new basilica had just begun.

Despite its aging condition, St. Peter's remained one of the most important pilgrimage destinations. The tomb of St. Peter beneath the high altar was the focal point, where pilgrims gathered to pray, seeking spiritual renewal and indulgences. Many relics and mosaics in the basilica drew visitors from across Europe. The decision to rebuild St. Peter's Basilica came during the papacy of Pope Julius II, after the Jubilee of 1500, with work starting in 1506.

The Sistine Chapel

In 1500, access to the Sistine Chapel was still highly restricted. The space is still revered as the Pope's private chapel. You hear whispers of its beauty but know that it remains a mystery to most pilgrims, symbolizing the layers of divine mystery within the Church.

During the 1500 Jubilee, the Sistine Chapel's walls were adorned with stunning frescoes, mostly finished by 1482, but the ceiling was just blue with stars. These frescoes were primarily created by renowned artists such as Sandro Botticelli, Domenico Ghirlandaio, Pietro Perugino, Cosimo Rosselli, and others. The fresco cycle depicted important biblical stories and served a dual purpose: to convey theological and doctrinal lessons while also celebrating the authority of the papacy. Rome in 1500 is a city amid Renaissance transformation. Great artists and thinkers fill its streets, contributing to a cultural revival.

The ultimate goal of your pilgrimage is to visit Rome's four major basilicas, passing through their Holy Doors to receive the plenary indulgence: St. Peter's Basilica, St. John Lateran, St. Mary Major, and St. Paul Outside the Walls. The journey to each is filled with prayer, awe, and reverence. These churches, deeply connected to the history of the faith, serve as key pilgrimage sites.

Art and Culture

While your pilgrimage is a spiritual journey, it also immerses you in Rome's flourishing culture. Every piazza, church, and corner of the city reflects the renaissance of Christian art and thought. The works of Botticelli and Perugino fill the churches, bringing Biblical stories to life in vivid detail.

1500 Jubilee Reflection

As your pilgrimage ends, you leave with a renewed sense of faith and a deeper understanding of the Renaissance spirit. The Jubilee of 1500 united the sacred and artistic, transcending time and space. You depart with memories of ancient basilicas, sacred art, and the faithful from all over Christendom, united in their devotion to the Church.

A Pilgrim's Journey to Rome: The Jubilee of 1650

As you approach the Eternal City in the mid-17th century, your heart races with anticipation. The Rome pilgrimage is both spiritual and sensory as you arrive at your destination.

First Glimpse of Rome

As Rome comes into view, you're struck by the sight of the ancient Aurelian Walls, built in the 3rd century AD. Rome's long history is evident in the massive fortifications encircling the city. However, your destination - St. Peter's Basilica and the Vatican area - lies outside these walls, on the west bank of the Tiber.

Unlike in future times, the area within the Leonine Walls is not strictly controlled. In 1650, the Borgo thrives as an integrated neighborhood. Pilgrims, locals, and clergy move freely through the gates, particularly the imposing Porta San Pietro, which serves as the main entrance to the Vatican area from the east.

Inside these walls, you find yourself in a dense urban landscape. The Borgo is filled with houses, shops, churches, and hospices catering to pilgrims. The streets are narrow and winding, typical of medieval urban planning. This area is very much alive and accessible, unlike the highly secured Vatican City of later times.

The concept of Vatican City as a sovereign state doesn't exist in 1650. The Pope rules a much larger territory covering much of central Italy, known as the Papal States. The Vatican area serves as the spiritual and administrative heart of this larger domain.

Entering the Eternal City in 1650

In 1650, during the Holy Year, most pilgrims from Europe entered Rome through the Porta del Popolo. This gate, located in the northern part of the city, was a main entry point for travelers arriving from the north, including those coming via the ancient Via Flaminia.

To honor the influx of pilgrims, Pope Alexander VII commissioned a redesign of the gate's interior in the mid-17th century by the architect Gian Lorenzo Bernini. The Porta del Popolo became a grand and welcoming entrance for pilgrims, symbolizing their arrival in the Eternal City and the start of their journey toward the major basilicas and holy sites.

From the east, your journey might bring you past the Baths of Diocletian. In 1561, Pope Pius IV commissioned Michelangelo to convert part of the frigidarium (the cold room of the baths) into a Catholic church, which became Santa Maria degli Angeli e dei Martiri. By 1650, this church was a prominent feature of the repurposed baths and is still an active church today. Michelangelo retained much of the monumental architecture of the original baths, including the large vaulted spaces, while adapting it for religious purposes.

Throughout Rome, fountains appear everywhere, fed by the restored Acqua Vergine aqueduct. The beautiful Fontana delle Tartarughe in Piazza Mattei, completed in 1588, exemplifies this abundance of water features.

A City of Faith

Religious orders form the backbone of pilgrim support. Benedictines in black robes, Franciscans in brown, Dominicans in white habits with black cloaks, and Jesuits in simple black cassocks move purposefully through the streets. Nuns and sisters of various orders add to the atmosphere of devotion, while behind convent walls, cloistered communities maintain constant prayer.

These orders actively care for pilgrims, operating hospices, providing spiritual guidance, and tending to the sick. The Franciscans and Dominicans offer clean accommodations, Jesuit priests hear confessions in multiple languages, and the Hospitaller Order of Saint John of God runs infirmaries throughout the city.

Churches associated with different orders serve as centers of activity. The Dominicans at Santa Maria sopra Minerva, the Jesuits at the Gesù, and the Franciscans at Santa Maria in Aracoeli host special services, provide accommodation, and offer spiritual guidance.

Approaching St. Peter's Basilica in 1650

The approach to St. Peter's reveals the contrast between the grand edifice and the dense urban fabric through which you navigate. Without the Via della Conciliazione (which won't exist for nearly three centuries), you wind through narrow, crooked medieval streets. The "Spina di Borgo" - a dense strip of medieval and Renaissance buildings - blocks any clear view until you're almost upon the basilica.

Emerging into the square, you find an irregularly shaped space, not yet transformed by Bernini's vision. The Egyptian obelisk, moved here in 1586, stands at the center. Buildings line the edges, providing shade but contributing to the somewhat chaotic feel of the space.

Inside St. Peter's Basilica in 1650

The basilica's interior, though unfinished, overwhelms with its grandeur. Michelangelo's dome allows sunlight to stream in, creating an almost heavenly atmosphere.

Notable works include:

Michaelangelo's Pietà, the Bronze Statue of St. Peter (its right foot worn from centuries of touches), the Navicella mosaic, the Tomb of Pope Paul III, and the Altar of St. Jerome.

The Navicella Mosaic is a large and historically significant mosaic originally created by Giotto di Bondone around 1305-1313 for the old St. Peter's Basilica in Rome. The mosaic depicts Jesus walking on water, reaching out to save the Apostle Peter, who is sinking. The name "Navicella," meaning "little ship" in Italian, refers to the central image of a boat, symbolizing the Church.

By 1650, the baldachin (or baldacchino) inside St. Peter's Basilica in Rome was already completed and well-established as one of the most iconic features of the church. The Baldacchino di San Pietro was designed by Gian Lorenzo Bernini and completed between 1624 and 1633, commissioned by Pope Urban VIII. This monumental bronze canopy stands over the high altar, which is situated directly above St. Peter's tomb.

Bernini's Baldachino in St. Peters was completed in 1634

The structure is made of bronze, with intricate baroque details, and stands approximately 30 meters (98 feet) tall. It marks the exact location of the papal altar and the site where St. Peter is believed to be buried. The baldachin's four twisted columns and their grand scale create a focal point in the vast interior of the basilica.

In 1650, it had become a prominent symbol of the papacy, as well as Bernini's genius, contributing to the overall grandeur of the basilica and enhancing the space's connection to the church's sacred history.

The lack of seating emphasizes the vastness of the space, as pilgrims move freely through the nave and side chapels.

The Sistine Chapel

Though closed to the public in 1650, the Sistine Chapel's reputation spreads through accounts of the fortunate few who have seen it. Michelangelo's ceiling frescoes and Last Judgment have achieved legendary status. While the Vatican Museums don't yet exist, the Vatican's art collection grows in papal apartments and palace corridors, though these remain private.

The Four Major Basilicas in 1650

Your pilgrimage takes you to the four major basilicas, each now resplendent in Renaissance and early Baroque glory:

Basilica di San Pietro / St. Peter's Basilica (Described above.)

Basilica di San Giovanni in Laterano / St. John Lateran

The most notable change to St. John Lateran was the transformation of its façade, completed during the Baroque period. The current façade was designed by Alessandro Galilei and completed in 1735, slightly later than the 1650 Jubilee. However, preparations and renovations for the 1650 Jubilee contributed to its Baroque appearance.

Earlier in the 1600s, Pope Sixtus V had already made significant changes to the church, including a new loggia and updates to the cloisters. The Baroque style brought grandeur, dynamism, and rich ornamentation that contrasted with the more austere medieval look that preceded it.

The interior also saw modifications, especially under Francesco Borromini, who was tasked with a major renovation by Pope Innocent X in preparation for the 1650 Jubilee. Borromini updated the nave with new stucco work, niches for statues of the apostles, and various decorative elements typical of the Baroque style, giving the basilica a more monumental and ornate feel.

Basilica di San Paolo Fuori le Mura / St. Paul Outside the Walls

Unlike many other churches in Rome, St. Paul Outside the Walls was not as heavily impacted by Baroque renovations during this period. The basilica still kept much of its early Christian architecture and layout. However, minor Baroque decorative updates were introduced, such as improvements to the altars, frescos, and some chapels, but the overall structure and design remained largely the same.

Basilica di Santa Maria Maggiore / Saint Mary Major

During the early 1600s, Pope Sixtus V initiated several significant projects, including the erection of the Sistine Chapel (not to be confused with the more famous Sistine Chapel in the Vatican), which is part of Santa Maria Maggiore and features a Baroque-style dome. This chapel, designed by Domenico Fontana, included the tomb of Sixtus V and was one of the important Baroque additions to the church.

Inside, the church saw more lavish stucco work, gilding, and new chapels that reflected the Baroque emphasis on grandeur and ornamentation. Frescos and altarpieces were also updated with Baroque aesthetics, emphasizing movement, emotion, and religious fervor. While the original cosmatesque floors and some early Christian mosaics were retained, Baroque artists and architects introduced more dynamic visual effects that were typical of the time.

Chapel of the Most Holy Sacrament in Santa Maria Maggiore

Chapel of the Holy Sacrament (Cappella del Santissimo Sacramento) in Santa Maria Maggiore, Rome. The chapel was completed in 1593, designed by the architect Flaminio Ponzio, with later additions by Girolamo Rainaldi.

The gilded bronze tabernacle at the center, visible in your image, was created by Lodovico del Duca. This magnificent tabernacle, modeled after the Temple of Jerusalem, serves as a repository for the Eucharist and is one of the highlights of the basilica's intricate interior design. The chapel is richly decorated with marble, gilding, and sculptures, befitting its importance as a place for Eucharistic adoration.

The New Churches of Rome in 1650

By 1650, Rome's skyline had been transformed by a collection of magnificent new churches that became the talk of the city, especially among the countless pilgrims who had never seen churches of this style.

These visitors marveled at the innovative Baroque churches with their dramatic facades and lavish ornamentation. Each architectural masterpiece stood as a testament to the flourishing new style, drawing admiring crowds of both locals and pilgrims who spread word of Rome's architectural wonders throughout Christendom. Here are some key examples:

Chiesa di Sant'Andrea della Valle

Begun in 1590 and completed in 1650, Sant'Andrea della Valle was very much a recent addition to the Roman cityscape in 1650. The church is particularly known for its impressive dome, which was, after St. Peter's, the second-largest in Rome at the time. Its lavish Baroque interior, especially the frescoed dome and the chapels, showcased the grandeur of this period.

The dome's frescoes, completed by Giovanni Lanfranco, and the richly decorated interior by Domenichino, were stunning new features that drew attention in the mid-17th century. The high altar was a focal point for pilgrims and visitors alike.

Il Gesù (Church of the Gesù)

Completed in 1584, Il Gesù was not as "new" in 1650 but was still considered modern for its innovative design. It was the mother church of the Society of Jesus (Jesuits) and had been a trendsetter for Baroque church architecture since its completion.

Il Gesù introduced the single nave plan, which became a model for many subsequent Baroque churches. The lavish interior, including Giovanni Battista Gaulli's dramatic ceiling fresco (though completed in the late 17th century), was a hallmark of the church. By 1650, pilgrims would have encountered its richly decorated chapels and impressive façade, which had set a standard for Baroque ecclesiastical design.

Chiesa di San Carlo alle Quattro Fontane (San Carlino)

Built by Francesco Borromini between 1638 and 1646, San Carlo alle Quattro Fontane (also called San Carlino) was a relatively new church in 1650 and represented a bold expression of Baroque architecture. Borromini's innovative, undulating façade and the intricate, geometrically complex interior made this small church a key Baroque masterpiece. Its compact yet highly dynamic design stood in contrast to the larger, more traditional basilicas.

Chiesa di Sant'Ignazio di Loyola

Built between 1626 and 1650, this Jesuit church dedicated to Saint Ignatius of Loyola was brand new by the 1650 Jubilee, with construction completed just in time. It was built to accommodate the growing influence of the Jesuits in Rome. Pilgrims in 1650 would already have been impressed by the monumental scale and the richly decorated interior of the church.

Chiesa di Santa Maria della Vittoria

Completed in 1620, Santa Maria della Vittoria was relatively new by 1650. Originally dedicated to St. Paul, it was rededicated to the Virgin Mary after the Catholic victory at the Battle of White Mountain in 1620. The church's interior exemplifies Baroque artistry, adorned with elaborate stucco, frescoes, and sculptures. Notably, it houses Gian Lorenzo Bernini's masterpiece, the Ecstasy of Saint Teresa, completed between 1647 and 1652. This sculpture, located in the Cornaro Chapel, depicts a mystical experience of Saint Teresa of Ávila and is celebrated for its dynamic composition and emotional depth.

Chiesa di Santissima Trinità dei Monti

Perched above the Spanish Steps, Santissima Trinità dei Monti was consecrated in 1585. Commissioned by King Louis XII of France in 1502, its construction spanned much of the 16th century. By 1650, the church was recognized for its French Gothic architecture, characterized by twin bell towers—a distinctive feature in Rome. The interior boasted significant artworks, including frescoes by Daniele da Volterra, a pupil of Michelangelo. The church's prominent location and artistic heritage made it a notable site during the Jubilee celebrations.

1650 Jubilee Reflection

As your journey through the Eternal City draws to a close, you pause to reflect on the transformation this pilgrimage has inspired. Rome, with its timeless grandeur, seems surprisingly modern, yet deeply rooted in its ancient faith. The city feels alive—a breathtaking fusion of religious devotion, artistic achievement, and human endeavor.

The grand basilicas, adorned with gilded ceilings and intricate mosaics, invite not only awe but a sense of closeness to the divine. These sacred spaces seem to pulse with the prayers of countless pilgrims who came before you, each seeking solace, penance, or inspiration. The magnificence of emerging Baroque art—its dynamic sculptures, vivid frescoes, and dramatic architecture—gives the sacred a tangible, almost theatrical presence. You are particularly struck by how these works of art do not merely depict faith but draw you into its very essence, stirring your heart with their emotional intensity.

The bustling piazzas and streets of Rome teem with life: vendors selling holy medals and rosaries, pilgrims recounting their spiritual encounters, and children playing in the shadows of centuries-old churches. Yet amidst this vitality, you sense an unseen undercurrent of prayer and charity. Behind the high walls of cloistered convents, nuns dedicate their lives to quiet contemplation and intercession. In nearby streets, members of religious orders feed the hungry, care for the sick, and offer a living example of Christ's teachings in action.

This Jubilee year has not just been a celebration; it has been a profound reminder of the Church's ability to unite the earthly and the divine. The ceremonies, indulgences, and solemn processions echo a faith that transcends time, renewing the weary soul. You leave Rome with a heart both humbled and uplifted, carrying the invisible presence of its faith-filled ecosystem within you. Rome, the center of Christendom, has reminded you not only of the glory of the Church but also of the enduring hope and strength found in the grace of pilgrimage.

CHAPTER ELEVEN

Giro delle Sette Chiese

The Pilgrimage of Rome's Seven Sacred Churches

A s the sun sets over Rome, a palpable sense of anticipation fills the air. The narrow cobblestone streets, bustling with tourists and locals alike, take on a unique character. Groups of pilgrims, some with candles in hand, others with rosaries wrapped around their fingers, gather. They are about to embark on a journey that has been undertaken for nearly five centuries: the Giro delle Sette Chiese or the Tour of the Seven Churches.

Soft streetlight glow illuminates determined faces preparing for the night pilgrimage. Some are local Romans, continuing a tradition passed down through generations. People from all over the world come here for the event's spiritual significance. As midnight approaches, a quiet excitement builds. Few tourists truly grasp the depth of Rome's history and spirituality.

This is not merely a tour of Rome's most famous basilicas. It is a journey through time and faith, a physical and spiritual odyssey that connects modern pilgrims with centuries of tradition. As we prepare to step onto this sacred path, we join countless others who have sought meaning, redemption, and connection on this very route.

Historical Roots: St. Philip Neri's Vision

The Giro delle Sette Chiese (the Walk of the Seven Churches) traces its origins to the mid-16th century and the visionary work of St. Philip Neri, known affectionately as the "Apostle of Rome." In 1551, at a time when the Church was facing significant challenges, and Rome itself was recovering from recent sackings, Neri saw an opportunity to revitalize faith through joyous, communal devotion.

Neri, the founder of the Oratory, a community dedicated to prayer and charitable works, envisioned a pilgrimage that would combine spiritual renewal with physical exercise and fellowship. His groundbreaking idea reimagined pilgrimages as celebrations of faith and community, rather than solemn acts of penance.

The Seven Basilicas: A Journey Through Rome's Sacred Heart

#1. Basilica di San Pietro (St. Peter's Basilica)

The history of St. Peter's Basilica stretches back to the dawn of Christianity. According to tradition, it stands on the site where St. Peter, the first pope, was martyred and buried in 64 AD. In 324 AD, Emperor Constantine ordered the construction of a basilica over St. Peter's tomb, a structure that stood for over a millennium.

The current basilica's story began in 1506 when Pope Julius II laid the foundation stone for a new church. The ambitious project spanned more than a century, involving some of the greatest artistic minds of the Renaissance. Donato Bramante provided the initial design, which was later modified by Michelangelo, who is credited with the iconic dome. The basilica was consecrated in 1626 by Pope Urban VIII. Its construction witnessed the artistic contributions of luminaries such as Raphael, Bernini, and Maderno, each leaving an indelible mark on this masterpiece of Renaissance and Baroque architecture.

Highlights

Michelangelo's Pietà: A Masterpiece of Renaissance Sculpture

In the first chapel on the right as you enter the basilica, Michelangelo's Pietà is one of the most celebrated sculptures in Western art. Created in 1499, this extraordinary work depicts the Virgin Mary cradling the lifeless body of Christ after the Crucifixion. Remarkable for its emotional depth, exquisite detail, and polished finish, the Pietà showcases Michelangelo's unparalleled mastery of marble. The tender expression on Mary's face and the naturalistic rendering of Christ's body make it a profoundly moving work. Protected behind bulletproof glass, the sculpture continues to inspire awe and devotion among visitors.

Bernini's Baldachin Over the Papal Altar

Standing beneath the central dome, Bernini's baldachin is a monumental canopy of gilded bronze that marks the location of St. Peter's tomb and the papal altar. Completed in 1634, the structure is over 28 meters (92 feet) tall and is an iconic example of Baroque art and architecture. Its twisted Solomonic columns are richly decorated with laurel leaves and bees, symbols of the Barberini family to which Pope Urban VIII, who commissioned the work, belonged. The baldachin creates a dramatic focal point under the dome, uniting the grandeur of St. Peter's Basilica with its sacred purpose as the heart of the Catholic Church.

The Tomb of St. Peter in the Necropolis Below the Basilica

Beneath the basilica lies the Scavi, the necropolis where St. Peter, one of Jesus Christ's twelve apostles and the first pope, is believed to have been buried. Archaeological excavations have revealed ancient tombs and a shrine marking the apostle's burial site. The highlight of this area is the aedicula, or small shrine, built to honor Peter. Pilgrims from around the world visit the necropolis to connect with the deep historical and spiritual roots of the Catholic Church. (**See the chapter on Visiting the Tomb of St. Peter for detailed visitor information.)

Michealangelo's Dome as seen from the rooftop

Climb to the Roof for Close-Up Views of Michelangelo's Dome

One of the most rewarding experiences at St. Peter's Basilica is the climb to the roof and dome. Visitors can take an elevator (only part of the way) or ascend a series of narrow, winding staircases to reach the roof, which offers panoramic views of Rome's skyline.

From here, you can admire the intricate details of Michelangelo's dome, one of the crowning achievements of Renaissance architecture. Designed in the 16th century, the dome's massive scale, harmonious proportions, and engineering brilliance have made it an enduring symbol of Rome and the Catholic Church. The climb also allows visitors to peer down into the basilica, offering a unique perspective of its grand interior.

Interior of Michaelangelos Dome of the Basilica di San Pietro

Did you know?

The basilica contains over 100 tombs, including those of 91 popes.

#2. Basilica di San Paolo Fuori le Mura

St. Paul Outside the Walls

The origins of St. Paul Outside the Walls date back to 324 AD when Emperor Constantine ordered a small chapel built over the tomb of St. Paul. This site, along the Via Ostiensis outside Rome's ancient walls, had been venerated by early Christians as the burial place of the Apostle to the

Gentiles. In 386, Emperor Theodosius I began the construction of a much larger and grander basilica, which was completed around 395.

Facade of the Basilica di San Paolo Fuori le Mura

This ancient basilica stood for nearly 1500 years, surviving countless wars and invasions. However, on the night of July 15, 1823, a fire accidentally started by a workman repairing the lead of the roof almost destroyed the church. The tragedy sparked a worldwide response. Global donations poured in, enabling the faithful reconstruction of the basilica in its original design.

The new St. Paul Outside the Walls was consecrated in 1854 by Pope Pius IX. Despite the reconstruction, the basilica keeps its original character as a paleochristian church, offering visitors a glimpse into the architectural style of early Christianity.

Highlights

The Chain of St. Paul

One of the most sacred relics housed in the basilica is the chain believed to have bound St. Paul during his imprisonment in Rome. This iron chain is displayed near the high altar, allowing visitors to reflect on the apostle's faith and endurance in the face of persecution. According to tradition, Paul was held in Mamertine Prison before his martyrdom and remained steadfast in his missionary work despite his suffering. The chain serves as a tangible connection to the life of one of Christianity's greatest figures and draws countless pilgrims each year seeking inspiration and spiritual renewal.

Stunning Mosaic of Christ Surrounded by the 24 Elders of the Apocalypse

The apse mosaic, completed in the 13th century, is one of the most awe-inspiring features of the basilica. It depicts Christ in Majesty, seated on a throne, with His right hand raised in blessing. Surrounding Him are the 24 elders of the Apocalypse, each holding golden crowns, symbolizing their worship of Christ as described in the Book of Revelation. The mosaic's rich gold background, intricate details, and vibrant colors make it a visual masterpiece of medieval Byzantine-style art. This mosaic not only reflects the basilica's grandeur but also invites visitors to contemplate the divine.

Portrait Medallions of All the Popes

Lining the walls of the nave are the famous portrait medallions depicting all the popes from St. Peter to the present day. This visual record of papal succession is unique to the Basilica of St. Paul Outside the Walls and underscores its historical importance within the Catholic Church. Each medallion features the pope's likeness along with their name and dates of their papacy. Tradition holds that when the last medallion is filled, the end of the world will come, adding an air of mystery and prophecy to this feature. Visitors often marvel at the continuity of leadership these portraits represent, a testament to the enduring legacy of the Church.

The Interior of the Basilica di San Paolo Fuori le Mura

Did you know?

In 2006, archaeologists confirmed the presence of a sarcophagus beneath the altar, believed to contain the remains of St. Paul.

#3. Basilica di San Giovanni in Laterano

St. John Lateran

Our third stop, the Basilica of St. John Lateran, holds the distinction of being the oldest of Rome's four major basilicas and the official ecclesiastical seat of the Pope as Bishop of Rome. Its history begins in the early 4th century when Emperor Constantine donated the Lateran Palace, formerly belonging to the noble Lateran family, to Pope Miltiades. Constantine then commissioned a grand basilica to be built next to the palace, which was consecrated by Pope Sylvester I in 324 AD. This consecration marked the foundation of the first Christian cathedral in Rome and the center of the Church's global authority.

Over the centuries, St. John Lateran faced many challenges. It was damaged by an earthquake in 897, sacked by invaders in 1308, and ravaged by fires in

1360 and 1361. Each time, the basilica was restored and often expanded. In the late 16th century, Pope Sixtus V oversaw a major renovation, and in 1646, Pope Innocent X commissioned Francesco Borromini to give the interior its current Baroque appearance.

Facade of the Basilica di San Giovanni in Laterano

The imposing facade, designed by Alessandro Galilei, was added in 1735 during the papacy of Pope Clement XII. This facade, with its massive Corinthian columns and distinctive Loggia of Benedictions, symbolizes the basilica's role as the "Mother of All Churches." Despite these changes, St. John Lateran remains a testament to the enduring power of the papacy and the resilience of Rome's Christian heritage.

The Lateran Baptistry

One of the most significant features of St. John Lateran is the Lateran Baptistry, located adjacent to the basilica. Constructed in the 4th century under Constantine, this is the oldest baptistry in the Christian world and set the architectural precedent for all subsequent baptistries.

Baptismal Font of the Lateran Baptistry

The octagonal building, surrounded by eight porphyry columns, reflects early Christian symbolism—the number eight representing resurrection and renewal.

The central font, believed to have originally been a Roman bath, was adapted for baptisms, signifying spiritual cleansing. By the Jubilee of 1650, the Lateran Baptistry had already undergone several enhancements, including mosaics, marble decorations, and chapels dedicated to Saint John the Baptist and Saint John the Evangelist. This site served as the primary location for baptisms in early Christian Rome, underscoring its foundational role in the sacramental life of the Church.

Loggia of Blessings San Giovanni in Laterano

The distinctive central balcony, known as the Loggia of Benedictions, is visible in this closer view, along with the massive Corinthian columns and the Latin inscription that identifies the basilica. These features are part of Alessandro Galilei's Baroque redesign completed in 1735 during Pope Clement XII's papacy. This façade is an iconic feature of the basilica and serves as the ceremonial platform for papal blessings.

Highlights

The Scala Santa (The Holy Stairs)

According to tradition, these are the steps Jesus ascended during His trial before Pontius Pilate in Jerusalem. They were brought to Rome by St. Helena in the 4th century and are a focal point for pilgrimages.

Cosmatesque Floor

The intricately patterned marble floor, a hallmark of medieval Roman churches, is a stunning example of geometric artistry.

Cosmatesque Floor Design

The Gothic Baldachin

Housing relics of Saints Peter and Paul, this 14th-century canopy rises above the main altar, symbolizing the continuity of apostolic succession.

Did you know?

Despite being in Rome and several miles from the Vatican, St. John Lateran is technically on sovereign Vatican territory. It is considered the spiritual and administrative center of the Catholic Church, even above St. Peter's Basilica.

#4. Basilica di Santa Maria Maggiore

St. Mary Major

The Basilica of St. Mary Major, one of Rome's four papal basilicas, has a history steeped in legend and devotion. According to tradition, the Virgin Mary appeared simultaneously to Pope Liberius and a wealthy Roman patrician named John in a dream on the night of August 4-5, 352 AD. She requested that a church be built in her honor on a site that would be marked by snow. Miraculously, snow fell on Esquiline Hill the next morning, outlining the area for the future basilica. This event is still celebrated on August 5 with the "Miracle of the Snow" feast.

Construction of the original basilica began shortly after this event. It was completed under Pope Sixtus III (432-440 AD), making it one of the oldest churches dedicated to the Virgin Mary in the world. Over the centuries, St. Mary Major has undergone many renovations and expansions, each adding to its splendor.

The 12th century saw the addition of the Romanesque bell tower, while the 14th and 15th centuries brought Renaissance and Baroque elements.

The basilica's most famous feature, its coffered ceiling, was gilded with gold, said to be from the first shipments from the Americas, commissioned by Pope Alexander VI in 1492. Throughout its history, St. Mary Major has remained a center of Marian devotion and a testament to Rome's enduring faith.

*Coffered ceiling of the Basilica
di Santa Maria Maggiore*

Highlights

5th-Century Mosaics Depicting Scenes from the Old Testament

One of the most remarkable features of Santa Maria Maggiore is its breathtaking 5th-century mosaics, among the oldest and most significant in Christian art. Stretching along the nave and triumphal arch, these mosaics depict vivid scenes from the Old Testament, such as the journey of Abraham, the Exodus, and the covenant with Moses. The rich details, vibrant colors, and golden backgrounds create a celestial atmosphere, embodying the early Christian church's artistic splendor.

The Crypt of the Nativity: Relic of Christ's Manger

Beneath the main altar lies the Crypt of the Nativity, home to a sacred relic believed to be fragments of the wooden manger that cradled the infant Jesus. Encased in a beautiful reliquary designed by Giuseppe Valadier, the relic is a focal point for pilgrims, especially during the Christmas season. The crypt is illuminated with soft lighting, highlighting the ornate design and inviting visitors to reflect on the mystery of Christ's birth.

The Borghese Chapel and the Miraculous Icon of the Virgin and Child

The Borghese Chapel, also known as the Pauline Chapel, houses the revered icon Salus Populi Romani ("Protectress of the Roman People"). This miraculous image of the Virgin and Child is attributed to Saint Luke and has been a symbol of Roman devotion for centuries. The chapel itself is an architectural and artistic masterpiece, featuring lavish marble, gilded stucco, and frescoes. Popes often pray here before significant events, reinforcing its importance in Catholic tradition.

The Coffer Ceiling: Gold from the Americas

The basilica's coffered ceiling is a masterpiece of Renaissance art, created during the papacy of Alexander VI. According to tradition, the gold used to gild the ceiling was the first brought to Europe from the Americas, gifted by the Spanish monarchy after Christopher Columbus's voyages. The shimmering panels reflect the wealth, artistry, and global reach of the Church during the Renaissance.

The Tomb of Gian Lorenzo Bernini

Gian Lorenzo Bernini, the legendary Baroque sculptor and architect, is buried in a simple family tomb near the basilica's baptistery. Known for masterpieces such as the Ecstasy of Saint Teresa and the colonnades of St. Peter's Square, Bernini left an indelible mark on Rome's artistic heritage. His burial in Santa Maria Maggiore reflects his deep faith and connection to the city. Visitors often pause at the site to honor his genius and legacy.

Baldachino and Mosaics of the Basilica di Santa Maria Maggiore

Did you know?

Every August 5th, a special Mass commemorates the "Miracle of the Snow" with white rose petals dropped from the ceiling.

#5. Basilica di San Lorenzo Fuori le Mura

St. Lawrence Outside the Walls

The Basilica of St. Lawrence Outside the Walls, our fifth stop, stands as a monument to one of the most revered martyrs of the early Christian church. Its history begins in the 4th century when Constantine I built a small oratory over the burial place of St. Lawrence, a deacon martyred in 258 AD during the persecution of Emperor Valerian. This original structure formed the basis of what would become one of Rome's most important pilgrimage sites.

In the 6th century, Pope Pelagius II significantly expanded the basilica, creating a new church that incorporated the older shrine. This expansion marked the beginning of centuries of development and renovation. In the 13th century, Pope Honorius III ordered another major reconstruction, essentially building a new church in front of the existing one and reversing its orientation. This unique architectural evolution resulted in the basilica's distinctive 'double church' layout.

Despite suffering damage during World War II bombings in 1943, the basilica was faithfully restored, preserving its rich mosaics, frescoes, and architectural elements that span nearly two millennia of Christian history.

Highlights

The Tomb of St. Lawrence

Located in the crypt beneath the basilica, the tomb of St. Lawrence is a revered pilgrimage site for Christians. St. Lawrence, one of the most venerated Roman martyrs, was executed during the persecution of Emperor Valerian in 258 AD. Visitors can view the tomb through a protective glass enclosure, which is illuminated to reveal the intricate carvings and reverent atmosphere of the crypt. The space invites quiet reflection and prayer.

13th-Century Cosmatesque Cloister

The cloister, designed in the distinctive Cosmatesque style, showcases the artistic genius of Roman marble workers from the 13th century.

The intricate geometric patterns of inlaid stone create a mesmerizing mosaic of colors, while the surrounding arcades feature beautifully carved columns and capitals. As a serene courtyard amidst the bustling city, the cloister offers a peaceful retreat for visitors to admire its craftsmanship and historical significance.

6th-Century Byzantine Mosaics in the Triumphal Arch

The triumphal arch of the basilica is adorned with a stunning series of Byzantine mosaics from the 6th century, making it one of the oldest surviving decorations in the church. These mosaics depict scenes from the life of the Virgin Mary and various biblical events, including the Annunciation and the Nativity. The gold background and vibrant colors reflect the light beautifully, creating a sense of divine radiance and emphasizing the basilica's role as a place of worship.

The Stone Gridiron of St. Lawrence

Legend holds that the stone gridiron displayed within the basilica was the very instrument of St. Lawrence's martyrdom. According to tradition, St. Lawrence was roasted alive on a gridiron as punishment for his defiance of Roman authorities. This relic serves as a powerful reminder of his faith and sacrifice, drawing the devotion of countless visitors. Its placement within the basilica underscores the connection between the church and the early Christian martyrs.

Did you know?

The basilica houses a stone slab with a large stain, believed by some to be from St. Lawrence's martyrdom.

#6. Basilica di Santa Croce in Gerusalemme

Holy Cross in Jerusalem

The Basilica of the Holy Cross in Jerusalem traces its origins to the early 4th century and is intimately connected with St. Helena, mother of Emperor Constantine. Around 325 AD, Helena embarked on a pilgrimage to the Holy Land, where she is said to have discovered relics of Christ's Passion, including fragments of the True Cross. Upon her return to Rome, she converted a room of her imperial palace, the Sessorian Palace, into a chapel to house these precious relics.

The chapel formed the core of the Basilica of the Holy Cross in Jerusalem. The name "in Jerusalem" refers not to its location but to the soil from Jerusalem that Helena had brought back and spread beneath the chapel's foundations, symbolically joining Rome to the Holy Land. Over the centuries, the basilica underwent several transformations. In the 12th century, it was given a Romanesque appearance, and in the 18th century, Pope Benedict XIV commissioned a major Baroque renovation. This renovation, completed in 1743, gave the basilica its current facade and much of its interior decoration. Despite these changes, the basilica retains its profound connection to early Christian history and continues to house some of the most venerated relics in Christendom.

Highlights

Chapel of Relics: Fragments of the True Cross

The Chapel of Relics is the heart of Santa Croce in Gerusalemme, housing sacred relics believed to be from the Passion of Christ. These include fragments of the True Cross, a thorn from the Crown of Thorns, a nail used in the Crucifixion, and a piece of the Titulus Crucis — the wooden plaque bearing the inscription "INRI" placed above Christ's head on the cross. These relics were brought to Rome by St. Helena, mother of Emperor Constantine, after her pilgrimage to the Holy Land in the 4th century. The chapel is a profoundly spiritual place, offering visitors a chance to connect deeply with the history and faith of Christianity.

Full-Size Replica of the Shroud of Turin

The basilica features an impressive, life-size replica of the Shroud of Turin, one of Christianity's most revered relics. While the original is kept in Turin, this detailed reproduction allows visitors to appreciate the mysterious image of a crucified man, believed by many to be Jesus Christ. The replica is displayed in a setting that invites contemplation on the Passion of Christ and the enduring mysteries surrounding the Shroud.

15th-Century Frescoes: The Legend of the True Cross

The basilica's interior is adorned with stunning 15th-century frescoes that depict the Legend of the True Cross. These artworks narrate the story of how St. Helena discovered the True Cross in Jerusalem, emphasizing her devotion and the miraculous events associated with the relics. The vibrant colors, expressive figures, and intricate details make these frescoes a significant artistic treasure, blending faith and history.

Baroque Façade Added in the 18th Century

The current façade of Santa Croce in Gerusalemme was designed by architect Pietro Passalacqua in the mid-18th century, transforming the basilica into a Baroque masterpiece. Its grand design features a two-story structure adorned with pilasters, statues, and elegant curves. The façade harmonizes beautifully with the basilica's ancient and medieval interior, creating a striking combination of architectural styles that reflect its long and evolving history.

#7. Basilica di San Sebastiano Fuori le Mura

St. Sebastian Outside the Walls

Our final stop, the Basilica of St. Sebastian Outside the Walls, holds a unique place in the topography of Christian Rome. Its origins date back to the mid-3rd century, when a small memorial was erected over the Ad Catacumbas, an underground burial complex. This site gained particular significance in Christian tradition, as it was believed to have temporarily housed the remains of Saints Peter and Paul during the persecutions of Emperor Valerian in 258 AD.

In the early 4th century, a basilica was constructed over this site, initially dedicated to the apostles Peter and Paul and known as the Basilica Apostolorum. It wasn't until the 9th century that the church was rededicated to St. Sebastian, a Roman soldier martyred during the persecution of Diocletian. The basilica underwent significant renovations in the 13th century under Pope Honorius III and again in the 17th century when Cardinal Scipione Borghese commissioned a complete reconstruction. This Baroque renovation, completed in 1611, gave the basilica much of its current appearance.

Despite these changes, St. Sebastian Outside the Walls remains deeply connected to its early Christian roots, particularly through its association with the extensive catacombs beneath it, which continue to attract pilgrims and scholars alike.

Highlights

Catacombs Beneath the Church

The catacombs of San Sebastiano are among the most significant in Rome, offering a profound connection to the early Christian community. These subterranean tunnels, originally used as a burial site for pagans and later Christians, house miles of intricate passages lined with tomb niches. Visitors can see early Christian graffiti, symbols of faith, and inscriptions that reveal the devotion of the first believers. The catacombs were named after St. Sebastian, who was originally buried here, making it a revered pilgrimage site. Walking through these ancient corridors provides a moving glimpse into the lives, struggles, and faith of early Christians under Roman persecution.

Relics of St. Sebastian

The basilica preserves several relics of St. Sebastian, one of the most venerated Roman martyrs. Among them is an arrow said to have been used in his attempted execution, as well as fragments of his body. St. Sebastian, a Roman soldier, was tied to a tree and shot with arrows for his Christian faith. Although he survived this ordeal, he was later executed by being beaten to death. His relics are enshrined in the basilica and serve as a reminder of his unwavering faith and martyrdom. Pilgrims often pray here, seeking his intercession for protection and strength.

The "Domine Quo Vadis" Stone

One of the most fascinating artifacts in the basilica is the "Domine Quo Vadis" stone, a slab of marble believed to bear the footprints of Jesus Christ. According to legend, Jesus appeared to St. Peter on the Via Appia as the apostle was fleeing persecution in Rome. When Peter asked, "Domine, quo vadis?" ("Lord, where are you going?"), Christ replied He was going to Rome to be crucified again. This encounter inspired Peter to return and face martyrdom. The footprints on the stone are a tangible symbol of this profound moment and are displayed as a relic of great spiritual significance.

The Albani Chapel

The Albani Chapel, designed by the renowned artist and architect Carlo Maratta in the late 17th century, is a Baroque masterpiece. Dedicated to the Virgin Mary, the chapel features elegant marble work, gilded stucco, and a serene statue of the Madonna and Child. The harmonious design of the chapel reflects Maratta's skill in combining classical and Baroque elements, creating a space that inspires devotion and awe. The chapel also contains several notable frescoes and paintings that add to its artistic and spiritual richness.

Did you know?

The Basilica of San Sebastiano Fuori le Mura is 7 kilometers (4.3 miles) from the Basilica of San Pietro.

The Living Tradition

Today, the Giro delle Sette Chiese continues to attract pilgrims and visitors from all corners of the globe. While traditionally associated with specific holy days, many now undertake this journey throughout the year, especially during the celebrations.

As dawn breaks after a night of pilgrimage, those who have completed the Giro delle Sette Chiese often describe a profound sense of spiritual renewal. The physical challenge of the journey, combined with the rich spiritual and historical significance of each stop, creates an experience that resonates far beyond the pilgrimage itself.

The Giro delle Sette Chiese is more than a tour of Rome's most sacred sites. It is a living tradition, a physical prayer, and a journey through the heart of Christian faith in the Eternal City.

For More Information:

- The Diocese of Rome is likely to provide information about organized pilgrimages, religious events, and significant celebrations, especially during important periods like Lent or the Jubilee Year. Check their official website for updates: https://www.diocesidiroma.ithttps://www.vaticannews.va

- The Opera Romana Pelligrinaggi (ORP) specializes in organizing pilgrimages in Rome and the Vatican. They frequently manage and promote the Giro delle Sette Chiese, especially for groups. Check their website for current or upcoming pilgrimage opportunities: https://www.operaromanapellegrinaggi.org

- The Vatican's official website may list events and pilgrimages, particularly during Jubilee Years or major religious celebrations. https://www.diocesidiroma.ithttps://www.vaticannews.va

If the Giro is not available during an evening when you are in Rome, it is still a glorious adventure during the daylight!

CHAPTER TWELVE

Visiting the Tomb of Saint Peter

The Vatican Scavi

V isiting the Tomb of St. Peter, beneath St. Peter's Basilica in Vatican City, is a spiritually significant and historically enriching experience. The tomb lies within the Scavi (excavations) beneath St. Peter's Basilica, in the Vatican Necropolis, an ancient burial site.

Plan and book your visit ahead to maximize this extraordinary opportunity. Opportunities to be a part of this tour are extremely limited.

Why Visit St. Peter's Tomb?

St. Peter's Tomb is a revered Christian pilgrimage site, believed to be the ultimate resting place of St. Peter, one of Jesus' apostles and the first Pope. The necropolis tour also offers an immersive experience, guiding visitors through ancient burial sites and fascinating archaeological finds from the early Christian period. It is a holy site and pilgrims should visit if they can reserve a spot.

Booking Your Visit in Advance

To visit the Scavi and the Tomb of St. Peter, you must book in advance as entry is highly restricted. Here's how to book:

Online Request

- The Vatican Scavi office handles all reservations. You can book directly through the Vatican's official website. High demand and limited space require making tour reservations months in advance.

- Visit the Vatican Excavations Office (Scavi) official website and submit a request form for your desired dates.

- You'll need to provide details like your preferred language, the number of participants, and your availability. The tours are often given in small groups of 12-15 people.

Once your request is approved, you will receive a confirmation email with further instructions on payment and final details.

Cost: The tour costs approximately €13-15 per person, depending on the current exchange rate and tour specifics.

Age Restrictions: Note that children under 15 are not allowed on the Scavi tour because of the delicate nature of the archaeological site and space constraints. I will say that in order to make this work when we had our young son traveling with us, we went separately. I booked myself Wednesday and my husband Thursday. It is an incredible trip through time under the Basilica. I highly recommend it.

What to Expect During the Tour

The Scavi Tour is led by experts, our guide was an archeologist, lasts about 90 minutes and will take you deep beneath St. Peter's Basilica, where you'll walk through ancient Roman mausoleums, early Christian burial chambers, and finally, to the Tomb of St. Peter.

Due to the humid and confined space, please dress comfortably, bring a jacket in the necropolis. Modest attire is required, as with all Vatican tours, meaning shoulders and knees should be covered.

Tours are available Monday through Saturday, usually between 9:00 AM and 5:00 PM. It's best to book as far in advance as possible.

- **Arrive early:** Enter Vatican City at least 15 minutes before your scheduled tour to pass through security without rushing. Plus when you are waiting to meet the guide you are inside of the Vatican and you can look around a bit while you wait. We found a cemetery!

- **Combine your visit:** Consider booking the Scavi tour on the same day as a visit to St. Peter's Basilica and the Vatican Museums, as they are all within the same area. However, keep in mind that you cannot re-enter the Basilica directly from the necropolis.

- Photos are not allowed in the building or on the tour.

By planning ahead and securing a spot on the Scavi tour, you'll have the unforgettable experience of walking in the footsteps of history.

Spiral Staircase of the Vatican Museum

CHAPTER THIRTEEN

Walking Tour: From Markets to Mosaics

Campo dei Fiori, Piazza Navona, Baroque Churches, and Mosaics

A Journey From Baroque Rome, Across the River to Trastavere

As you embark on this enchanting journey through some of Rome's most charming neighborhoods, prepare to immerse yourself in the city's vibrant culture, fascinating stories, and breathtaking views.

This self-guided walking tour, covering approximately 4 km (2.5 miles), begins at the lively Campo de' Fiori and concludes across the river in Trastavere.

#1. Campo de' Fiori

Start your day with a coffee or light breakfast near Campo de' Fiori, where you'll begin your adventure. As you enter the square, you'll be greeted by a bustling morning market.

Take your time to wander among the colorful stalls, filled with fresh produce, fragrant flowers, and local specialties. At the center of the square, observe the statue of Giordano Bruno, a somber reminder of the area's complex history.

Beautiful produce at the morning market
in Campo di Fiori

Breakfast recommendation: My favorite coffee and pastry spot near Campo de Fiori is Pasticceria Riscioli. It's a quick walk from the campo. The Pasticceria offers bar service and seating outside. The pastries are top-notch.

*Coffee and
the delights of
Pasticceria Riscioli*

#2. Piazza Navona

The magnificent Piazza Navona stretches across what was once the ancient Stadium of Domitian, where Romans once cheered chariot races and athletic contests. Today, this elegant baroque showcase preserves the exact shape of that ancient arena, though its present grandeur stems from the mid-17th century when the Pamphili family transformed it into Rome's most theatrical public space. At its center, Bernini's Fountain of the Four Rivers rises like a massive sculpture garden, where river gods represent the known continents, crowned by an ancient Egyptian obelisk that seems to defy gravity as it soars toward the sky.

Flanking this centerpiece are two other fountains that mark the piazza's ends: the Fountain of the Moor to the south, also touched by Bernini's hand, and the Fountain of Neptune to the north, added later to create perfect symmetry. Dominating the western side stands the Church of Sant'Agnese in Agone, its concave facade by Borromini engaging in an eternal dialogue with Bernini's fountain just across the square. The church rises from the very spot where the young Saint Agnes was said to have been martyred, its dome and twin bell towers creating one of Rome's most memorable architectural profiles.

The surrounding palaces, including the imposing Palazzo Pamphili, complete this outdoor theater where baroque art and architecture perform their endless show for visitors who might sit at a cafe table or strolling across the piazza's cobblestones, just as Romans have done for centuries.

#3. Sant'Andrea delle Valle (St. Andrew of the Valley)

One of my favorite churches of Rome is located a 4-minute walk from Campo de Fiori. Sant'Andrea delle Valle is a magnificent example of Baroque architecture.

Built with the support of Cardinal Alessandro Peretti di Montalto in 1590, this church became the spiritual heart of the Theatine Order. Its monumental dome, one of the largest in Rome and second only to St. Peter's Basilica, dominates the skyline and is a testament to the engineering mastery of its time.

As you approach, you'll be struck by the grandeur of the façade, completed in the mid-17th century by Carlo Rainaldi. Inside, the church is a masterpiece of Baroque art, richly adorned with frescoes by Domenichino and Giovanni Lanfranco, whose works illuminate the apse and dome. This artistic richness, combined with the church's significant role during the Counter-Reformation, makes Sant'Andrea della Valle a key site for understanding the evolution of Baroque religious art.

Golden baroque ceiling of Sant'Andrea

History of Sant'Andrea della Valle

The church's construction began in 1590 under the patronage of Cardinal Alessandro Peretti di Montalto, the nephew of Pope Sixtus V. The site was previously occupied by an earlier church dedicated to Saint Sebastian, which was granted to the Theatine Order. The Theatines, a religious order founded in 1524 to reform the clergy and fostering the spirit of the Counter-Reformation, needed a new church for their growing congregation.

The initial design of Sant'Andrea della Valle was by Giacomo della Porta, one of the leading architects of the late Renaissance. After his death, the work was continued by Carlo Maderno, a key figure in early Baroque architecture, who is also known for his work in St. Peter's Basilica. Maderno redesigned the plan to include one of the largest domes in Rome, completed by Francesco Borromini.

The façade, completed in the mid-17th century, was designed by Carlo Rainaldi, another prominent Baroque architect. The façade is a striking example of Baroque grandeur, with its powerful verticality, dynamic forms, and rich ornamentation.

The church was consecrated in 1650 by Pope Innocent X. It has been associated with various papal ceremonies and has maintained its importance within the Theatine Order and the broader Roman Catholic Church.

The dome of Sant'Andrea della Valle is one of the largest in Rome, second only to St. Peter's Basilica. The dome was designed by Carlo Maderno and completed by Francesco Borromini. It stands at over 80 meters high and is a masterpiece of engineering and design. The interior of the dome is decorated with a magnificent fresco by Giovanni Lanfranco, depicting the "Glory of Paradise" with a swirling mass of angels and saints, creating a sense of movement and ascension.

The interior of the church follows a Latin cross plan with a long nave, side chapels, a transept, and a deep apse. The nave is wide and grand, leading the eye directly to the altar and the dome above. The architectural proportions and use of light contribute to the sense of verticality and spiritual elevation that characterizes Baroque church interiors.

The interior is richly decorated with frescoes and sculptures. The apse is adorned with a series of frescoes by Domenichino, depicting scenes from the life of Saint Andrew, including his martyrdom. These frescoes are celebrated for their dramatic composition and vibrant color palette, typical of Baroque art.

The high altar is another focal point, designed by Carlo Maderno, featuring a large altarpiece with a depiction of the Crucifixion of Saint Andrew (he was crucified on an X-shaped cross). Using gilding, rich marble, and detailed carvings throughout the church reflects the opulence and religious fervor of the Baroque era.

The side chapels of Sant'Andrea della Valle are each unique, with their own altars, paintings, and sculptures. Notable among these is the Cappella Barberini, which contains the tomb of Pope Urban VIII, a member of the powerful Barberini family. The chapels add to the overall richness and diversity of the church's interior.

High altar with St. Andrew on an X shaped cross

The church is a masterpiece of Baroque architecture and a significant historical site in Rome. Its towering dome, elegant façade, and richly decorated interior make it a must-visit for those interested in religious art and architecture. The church's history, closely tied to the Theatine Order and the Counter-Reformation, adds to its importance as a spiritual and cultural landmark in Rome.

As someone who has experienced the awe-inspiring beauty of this site firsthand, I wholeheartedly recommend a visit. When I stepped inside, I was immediately struck by the sheer grandeur of the space and the intricate details adorning every surface. The play of light through the windows, illuminating the frescoes and gilded decorations, created an atmosphere that was truly captivating.

Whether you're an art enthusiast, history buff, or simply someone who appreciates breathtaking architecture, I assure you that this stop will not disappoint. It offers a deeply rewarding experience that reflects the splendor and spiritual intensity of the Baroque era.

Standing beneath its magnificent dome, I felt transported to another time, gaining a profound appreciation for the skill and devotion of those who created this extraordinary place. Trust me, it's an experience you won't want to miss during your time in Rome.

#4. Chiesa del Gesù: The Jesuit Order's Baroque Jewel

Just a short 5-minute walk from Sant'Andrea della Valle lies another breathtaking masterpiece of Baroque architecture: the Chiesa del Gesù (Church of Jesus). Each time I visit, I'm captivated by its mesmerizing decoration, intense colors, and the way it embodies the grandeur and emotion of Baroque art. The interior is a veritable feast for the eyes, with gilded surfaces, intricate frescoes, and bold designs creating an atmosphere that is as awe-inspiring as it is moving.

Stepping inside, you're immediately enveloped in the vibrancy and richness of the space. Light interacts with the ornate ceiling, breathing life into the church. Every visit reveals something new, whether it's the shimmering of gold leaf or the details of a fresco you may have missed before. It's a church that continues to offer fresh discoveries no matter how many times you return.

More than just a stunning example of Baroque design, Chiesa del Gesù holds immense historical importance as the mother church of the Jesuit Order, making it central to the Catholic Counter-Reformation. Built in 1568 under the patronage of Cardinal Alessandro Farnese, grandson of Pope Paul III, the church was completed after Ignatius of Loyola's death, realizing his dream of establishing a grand Jesuit church.

Giacomo Barozzi da Vignola, a leading architect of the time, designed the initial structure, and after his death, Giacomo della Porta took over, completing the façade in 1575.

The façade itself is considered a landmark in architectural history, marking a transition from Renaissance to Baroque design. With its dynamic forms, paired pilasters, and dramatic use of space, it set the template for Jesuit churches worldwide, becoming a defining element of Baroque architecture.

Interior of The Gesù

To facilitate preaching and the celebration of Mass, crucial elements of the Jesuit mission, the church follows a layout based on the Latin cross, featuring a wide nave, side chapels, and an emphasis on the altar. Aiming to inspire awe and devotion, the lavish decoration reflects the ideals of the Counter-Reformation. The ceiling fresco, "Triumph of the Name of Jesus," by Giovanni Battista Gaulli (Baciccia), completed in 1679, is a stunning example of Baroque illusionism, where the heavens seem to open up and figures spill into the church, dissolving the boundary between the earthly and the divine.

Adorned with lapis lazuli, gilt bronze, and marble, the high altar, designed by Giacomo della Porta, is another focal point. The Altar of St. Ignatius, in the left transept, is a Baroque spectacle designed by Andrea Pozzo, featuring a statue of the saint alongside a giant lapis lazuli globe.

What I find most fascinating about Chiesa del Gesù is how it encapsulates both architectural and religious history. As the mother church of the Jesuits, it represents the order's commitment to education, evangelization, and global mission. It played a crucial role during the Counter-Reformation and remains a monument to Jesuit influence across the world.

Each visit brings additional details to light—the intricate symbolism, the expressive sculptures, and the powerful frescoes—making it a must-see for anyone interested in art, architecture, or religious history.

One thing I appreciate most is its accessibility. Unlike some churches with limited hours, Chiesa del Gesù is open daily, all day, offering plenty of opportunities to explore its splendor.

#5. Lunch at Antico Forno Roscioli or Across the River in Trastavere

After your visit to the Chiesa del Gesù, I have a treat in store for you I absolutely love, a double dose of Roscioli family deliciousness! Remember how I recommended Pasticceria Roscioli for breakfast? Now, let's try another branch of this talented culinary family for lunch.

Just a short walk from the church, you'll find Antico Forno Roscioli, the bakery side of the family business. Trust me, your taste buds are in for a real Roman feast here! This renowned bakery and deli, founded in 1972, has become a local institution, and for good reason.

Or Lunch in Trastavere: If you prefer to sit down in a restaurant for lunch I recommend crossing the river and having lunch at either Trattoria Da Enzo al 29 (closer to the Basilica of Santa Cecilia) or Osteria der Belli (closer to the Basilica of Santa Maria in Trastavere). Both offer traditional Roman cuisine.

#6. Basilica di Santa Maria in Trastevere

Mosaic of the dormition of the Virgin Mary

Crossing the Tiber River into the lively Trastevere district, your next stop is Santa Maria in Trastevere, one of the oldest Christian churches in Rome and a true gem of medieval art. Founded in the 4th century AD, this basilica is steeped in history, with its origins linked to the early Christian community in Rome. Retaining much of its medieval charm, the current structure, which was largely rebuilt in the 12th century by Pope Innocent II, also integrates elements from earlier periods.

The golden mosaics and the baldachin

Santa Maria in Trastevere is renowned for its stunning mosaics, especially those found in the apse. The apse mosaic, created by Pietro Cavallini, depicts the Coronation of the Virgin, one of the most magnificent examples of 13th-century Roman art. Scenes from the life of the Virgin Mary are depicted in the mosaics on the triumphal arch. The shimmering gold ceiling and the re-used ancient Roman columns in the nave further enhance the church's beauty, blending early Christian symbolism with later medieval artistry.

This church is not only a masterpiece of architecture and art, but it also symbolizes the resilience of Rome's Christian community throughout centuries of history. Its mosaics and sacred relics offer a fascinating glimpse into both medieval and early Christian Rome, making this church a must-see for any visitor interested in religious history and art.

#7. Basilica di Santa Cecilia in Trastevere

A short walk deeper into Trastevere brings you to Santa Cecilia in Trastevere, a church with a rich history tied to one of Christianity's most revered saints. The church is dedicated to Saint Cecilia, the patron saint of music, who was martyred in the 3rd century AD. In accordance with tradition, the church is on the site of her home, where she endured her martyrdom. The church was rebuilt in the 9th century by Pope Paschal I, and later restored, preserving its early Christian and medieval heritage.

Inside, you will find Stefano Maderno's famous sculpture of Saint Cecilia lying in repose beneath the main altar, a moving representation of the saint's martyrdom. The church's crypt holds relics of Saint Cecilia, offering a spiritual connection to the saint. The choir's frescoes, painted by Pietro Cavallini in the late 13th century, represent one of the earliest examples of Roman naturalism and provide a striking contrast to the more symbolic medieval mosaics seen elsewhere.

Roman Ruins

Visitors can also explore the ancient Roman ruins underneath the church, believed to be the remains of Saint Cecilia's house, providing yet another layer of historical depth to this already significant site. For those with an interest in early Christian history and art, Santa Cecilia in Trastevere offers a profound and serene experience, set within the vibrant surroundings of Trastevere.

From merchants haggling in morning markets to artists crafting masterpieces, from ancient stadium grounds to Baroque fountains, each step has revealed how Romans past and present have shaped these spaces. Our path across the Tiber brought us face-to-face with sacred architecture that continues to inspire awe, just as it did centuries ago. These neighborhoods, though each distinct, weave together to tell the story of a city where daily life, art, and faith have always intertwined, creating the vibrant tapestry that is Rome.

CHAPTER FOURTEEN

Ancient Rome Walking Tour

Walking in the Footsteps of the Emperors

As you embark on this journey through the heart of Ancient Rome, you'll walk in the footsteps of emperors, senators, and citizens who shaped the eternal city. This carefully crafted route takes you through nearly a millennium of Roman history, from the mighty Colosseum to the architectural wonder of the Pantheon. The walk covers approximately 3 kilometers (1.9 miles) and typically takes 4-5 hours, including visits inside the monuments.

Before you start, ensure you've purchased your combined ticket for the Colosseum, Roman Forum, and Palatine Hill in advance–this will save you considerable time.

The Colosseum

Your adventure begins at the Flavian Amphitheater, better known as the Colosseum. Standing before this magnificent structure, you'll understand why it has captivated visitors for nearly two millennia. Built between 70-80 AD under the Flavian emperors, this massive amphitheater could hold up to 50,000 spectators, all carefully arranged according to their social status–from slaves and foreigners in the upper wooden seats to senators in the front rows.

Explore the three levels of arches, each showcasing a different architectural order–Doric, Ionic, and Corinthian. The recently restored hypogeum reveals the complex underground system where gladiators and wild animals once waited before their appearances. The partial arena floor helps visitors visualize the spectacles that once took place here, from gladiatorial contests to mock sea battles.

*See Securing Tickets Chapter for additional information regarding Colosseum tickets.

Arch of Constantine and Palatine Hill

As you exit the Colosseum, pause at the Arch of Constantine. This triumphal arch tells a fascinating story of Roman artistic renewal and political propaganda. Built in 315 AD, it incorporates sculptures from earlier monuments, demonstrating how Roman emperors sometimes appropriated their predecessors' achievements to enhance their own legacy.

Ascending the Palatine Hill, you'll reach the birthplace of Rome itself. According to legend, this is where Romulus founded the city in 753 BCE. Home to emperors and aristocrats, the hill eventually became Rome's most exclusive neighborhood. Glimpses into the lavish lifestyle of Roman emperors are offered by the remains of several imperial palaces. The House of Augustus, with its well-preserved frescoes, provides intimate insights into the private life of Rome's first emperor. From the hill, admire sweeping views of the Circus Maximus and the Forum.

The Roman Forum

Descending into the Forum valley, you enter the pulsing heart of ancient Rome. This was where citizens gathered to conduct business, participate in religious ceremonies, attend criminal trials, and engage in politics. The Temple of Saturn, with its remaining columns, once housed the state treasury. Nearby, the House of the Vestal Virgins tells the story of Rome's sacred priestesses who maintained the eternal flame. The Basilica of Maxentius, with its towering vaults, demonstrates the engineering prowess of Roman architects.

The Arch of Titus, commemorating the conquest of Jerusalem, leads you toward the Curia Julia, where the Roman Senate met to govern their vast empire. The Temple of Antoninus and Faustina stands as a testament to imperial love, converted into a church that helped preserve its ancient structure. Explore freely, for each stone holds a tale, and history's layers are deep and intricate.

Capitoline Hill and Theater of Marcellus

Climbing the Michelangelo-designed steps to the Capitoline Hill, you reach Rome's sacred citadel. This smallest of Rome's seven hills played an outsized role in Roman religious and political life. The piazza, designed by Michelangelo, offers spectacular views of the Forum below and modern Rome beyond.

The Capitoline Museums

The museums are the world's oldest public museums, dating back to 1471 when Pope Sixtus IV donated a collection of bronze statues to the people of Rome. Housed in two main buildings, the Palazzo dei Conservatori and the Palazzo Nuovo, the museums feature a vast collection of ancient Roman, Greek, and Renaissance art.

These buildings are full of incredible sculptures, paintings, and archaeological treasures, including the Capitoline Wolf, the statue of Marcus Aurelius, and the iconic Dying Gaul. The museums provide a rich historical narrative of Rome, displaying artifacts that highlight the city's significance from its ancient roots to the Renaissance period.

Stunning high relief sculpture on sarcophagus in the museum

Besides its art collections, the Capitoline Museums offer visitors a chance to explore the stunning architecture of Michelangelo's piazza design, which unites the two palaces with the Cordonata, a grand staircase leading up to the square. The Palazzo Senatorio, situated between the two museum buildings, adds to the historical importance of the area, serving as the seat of the Roman city government.

The museums also offer panoramic views of the Roman Forum, allowing visitors to reflect on the ancient history that shaped the Eternal City. Together, the Capitoline Museums encapsulate Rome's enduring legacy, where art, politics, and history intertwine across centuries. Tickets can be purchased in advance: https://museiincomuneroma.vivaticket.it/

Largo di Torre Argentina and The Pantheon

The ruins at Largo di Torre Argentina offer a unique glimpse into Republican Rome. These four temples, discovered during 20th-century renovations, date from the Roman Republic's middle and late periods. This square also marks the approximate location where Julius Caesar was assassinated on the Ides of March, though the actual spot lies under a modern road nearby. Today, the ruins share space with a famous cat sanctuary, creating a uniquely Roman blend of ancient and modern life.

Your journey culminates at the magnificent Pantheon, Rome's best-preserved ancient monument and a remarkable testament to the ingenuity of Roman engineering. Originally built during Hadrian's reign around 126 AD, the Pantheon was dedicated to all Roman gods. It now serves as a Catholic church, officially known as the Basilica of St. Mary and the Martyrs (Santa Maria ad Martyres), reflecting its enduring legacy and transformation over centuries.

The massive dome remains the world's largest unreinforced concrete dome and features a striking open oculus at its center, allowing natural light and rain to enter the building, creating a unique, ever-changing atmosphere. The dome's perfect proportions—its height equals its diameter—demonstrate the Roman genius for harmonizing beauty and precision. Standing beneath the coffered ceiling, you can marvel at the geometric elegance that enhances the dome's structural integrity.

The Pantheon's grandeur extends to its original bronze doors, which still function today, and its richly decorated interior, a blend of ancient and Renaissance elements. Inside, you'll find a variety of chapels and altars added during its conversion to a church. These elements are adorned with marble, mosaics, and Christian iconography, blending the spiritual with the architectural.

Pantheon under a full moon

Among the Pantheon's most famous features are the tombs of Italian royalty and notable figures. King Victor Emmanuel II, the first king of a unified Italy, is interred here, alongside his son, King Umberto I, and Queen Margherita. The basilica is also the final resting place of the Renaissance master Raphael, whose epitaph reads: "Here lies Raphael, by whom Nature feared to be outdone while he lived, and when he died, feared she herself would die."

The Pantheon is more than just a preserved ancient monument; it is a living connection to Rome's rich history, combining its pagan roots, Christian legacy, and role as a national symbol.

CHAPTER FIFTEEN

Rome's Architectural Evolution Walking Tour

Ancient Rome, Medieval Rome, and Baroque Rome

Rome's architectural landscape serves as a living chronicle of the city's history and the progression of human innovation. From ancient structures showcasing engineering marvels to Renaissance masterpieces and Baroque innovations, this tour provides a journey through time, examining how each period influenced the city's built environment.

In each location, we'll observe the transition in architectural styles, construction methods, and design philosophies that define Rome's legacy as a world architectural capital. This full-day itinerary immerses you in the rich layers of Roman architecture, highlighting structural and aesthetic advancements across millennia. If you want to enjoy the archeological evolution of Rome, this is the tour for you.

Duration: Full Day (8-9 hours)

Tour Details and Stops

Morning: We'll begin with Ancient Rome, focusing on the enduring influence of Roman engineering and design in the Roman Forum, the Colosseum, and the Pantheon, each symbolizing different aspects of Rome's might and ingenuity.

Afternoon: Moving forward in time, we'll explore sites that represent the shift from medieval austerity to the balanced beauty of the Renaissance, including the intricate layers of the Basilica of San Clemente and the elegant proportions of the Palazzo della Cancelleria and Tempietto di San Pietro in Montorio.

Baroque Period: Our next stops include Baroque icons like the Church of Sant'Ivo alla Sapienza, where Borromini's creative genius shines, and the Palazzo Farnese, a Renaissance and Baroque masterpiece with its grandiose detailing and stately proportions.

And finally a visit to the Hall of Mirrors in the Galleria Doria Pamphili.

Morning: Ancient Rome

The Roman Forum

The Temple of Saturn dates back to around 497 BC (rebuilt in 42 BC), and it holds symbolic importance as one of the earliest monumental temples in Rome. The Basilica Julia, established by Julius Caesar and later modified by Augustus, reflects the Roman emphasis on judicial and civic life with its vast open spaces and multiple tribunal rooms. Also, consider including the Temple of Vesta and the House of the Vestal Virgins—notable for the round temple design and the role of Vestal Virgins in ancient Roman religion.

The Colosseum

The iconic amphitheater that hosted gladiatorial games and spectacles for up to 50,000 spectators, featuring a complex system of underground chambers and mechanical lifts that would bring animals and gladiators to the arena floor. The building's revolutionary design uses a precise combination of arches, vaults, and columns across four stories, with each level showcasing a different Classical order of architecture (Tuscan, Ionic, and Corinthian). Its ingenious design allowed crowds to enter and exit the massive structure in just minutes through 80 numbered entrances, while its sophisticated water drainage and ventilation systems made it a marvel of ancient engineering. The intricate system of corridors and passages beneath the arena floor, known as the hypogeum, operated like a complex theatrical machinery system, allowing for elaborate staged spectacles that would have amazed ancient audiences.

The Pantheon

This architectural marvel represents the pinnacle of Roman engineering and mathematical precision, where a perfect sphere resting in a cylinder creates harmonious proportions that have influenced architects for two millennia.

The massive dome spans 142 feet in diameter and reaches the same height from the floor, creating a perfect sphere that could contain a complete ball. Its revolutionary concrete composition becomes gradually lighter as it rises, using heavy aggregate at the base and lightweight pumice in the upper sections, while deep coffers in the ceiling reduce the weight without compromising structural integrity.

The 27-foot central oculus remains the building's engineering masterpiece, acting not only as a compression ring that stabilizes the dome but also creating a mesmerizing interplay of light that transforms the interior throughout the day and during different seasons.

The oculus of the Pantheon

The building's massive bronze doors, standing 24 feet high, are still the original Roman ones, while the elegant portico features 16 monolithic granite columns, each weighing 60 tons, transported from Egypt at enormous expense to create one of the most impressive entrances in ancient Rome.

The Pantheon's original bronze ceiling beams were removed by Bernini on orders from Pope Urban VIII in the 17th century to create the canopy in St. Peter's Basilica. This loss is a part of Rome's historical narrative, as it shows the city's practice of repurposing materials. Additionally, the Pantheon's portico and dome are one of the few structures from ancient Rome to remain largely intact, due in part to its conversion to a church in the 7th century.

Afternoon: Medieval to Renaissance

Basilica of San Clemente

A fascinating architectural layer cake that physically demonstrates Rome's historical stratification, where visitors descend through twelve centuries of history. The current 12th-century medieval church showcases a magnificent Byzantine-style apse mosaic and one of Rome's finest cosmatesque marble floors, created by medieval craftsmen using geometric patterns of colored stone.

Below this lies a perfectly preserved 4th-century basilica, its walls still adorned with rare medieval frescoes including unusual secular scenes and some of the first written examples of the Italian language.

Descending further, visitors discover a 1st-century Roman temple dedicated to Mithras, complete with marble seating and an altar showing the god slaying a bull, alongside a Roman apartment building (insula) with a working spring-fed fountain that still flows after 2,000 years. The different levels showcase distinct construction techniques, from Roman brick and concrete work to medieval stone masonry, providing a unique vertical timeline of architectural evolution.

Palazzo della Cancelleria

Palazzo della Cancelleria is considered one of Rome's first Renaissance palaces, built between 1485 and 1511. It exemplifies early Renaissance architecture in Rome with its harmonious proportions, rusticated stone base, and classical detailing. The façade's subtle use of pilasters and balanced windows reflect the Renaissance ideals of symmetry and balance. Michelangelo is rumored to have contributed to its courtyard design, which features arcades and graceful arches.

Tickets: Entry is generally free, though access may be limited as the building houses church administrative offices. It's best to check for any public opening hours in advance, as it occasionally hosts temporary exhibitions that may require a small fee.

Tempietto di San Pietro in Montorio

Designed by Donato Bramante in 1502, this "tempietto" (little temple) is one of the most perfect examples of High Renaissance architecture. Its circular form, based on classical temples, symbolizes harmony and balance. The Doric columns, proportionate design, and use of symmetry showcase Bramante's mastery and serve as a quintessential Renaissance reference, inspiring later architects like Michelangelo.

Tickets: Access to the Tempietto courtyard is free. However, if you wish to see the nearby Academy of Spain where it is located, you may need permission or a pre-arranged visit, as the area is often restricted.

Church of Sant'Ivo alla Sapienza

Designed by Francesco Borromini in the mid-17th century, Sant'Ivo alla Sapienza is an architectural gem of Baroque design. Its unique corkscrew dome is a marvel of Baroque creativity, symbolizing both the flame of the Holy Spirit and the ascent of human knowledge. The church's concave and convex curves create dynamic movement, and the innovative interior plan with a star shape emphasizes Borromini's mastery of geometry and symbolism in architecture.

Borromini's use of the star-shaped floor plan and the spiral dome reflect his innovative approach to Baroque design, breaking from traditional forms. The twisted spire is thought to symbolize both divine inspiration and the wisdom of Sapienza (knowledge), as the building was initially part of a university complex. The concave and convex forms of the building's exterior reflect Borromini's mastery of visual and spatial dynamism.

Tickets: No tickets are generally required. However, the church is only open during certain hours on Sundays and specific days for visits, so it's best to check opening times in advance if you'd like to see the interior.

Palazzo Farnese

Palazzo Farnese is one of the grandest Renaissance palaces in Rome, showcasing work by notable architects like Antonio da Sangallo the Younger and Michelangelo. Michelangelo added the third floor and designed the grand cornice, contributing to the palace's imposing and elegant Renaissance facade. The interior features a grand courtyard and frescoes by Annibale Carracci, making it a rich example of Renaissance architecture with contributions from multiple artistic masters.

Tickets: As the palace serves as the French Embassy, visits are limited and often require pre-arranged tours. The embassy occasionally opens for guided tours by reservation, which provide access to key rooms and the famous Carracci Gallery. Tickets for these tours are typically around €12–€15, and reservations are essential.

Galleria Doria Pamphilj

The Galleria Doria Pamphilj is located in the Palazzo Doria Pamphilj, a residence of the influential Doria Pamphilj family. Its origins date back to the 16th century, and over the years, the palace has been expanded and adorned to reflect the family's prestige. The art collection began in the 17th century under the patronage of Pope Innocent X Pamphilj and has remained one of the most significant private art collections in Rome.

What to See:

- Gallery of Mirrors: Inspired by the Hall of Mirrors at Versailles, this lavish room showcases gilded stucco, intricate frescoes, and mirrors that amplify its grandeur. It embodies the splendor and artistic ambition of the Baroque era.

Hall of Mirrors in the Galleria Doria Pamphili

- Art Collection: The gallery features masterpieces by renowned artists such as Caravaggio, Velázquez, Titian, and Raphael. Highlights include Velázquez's celebrated portrait of Pope Innocent X and Caravaggio's "Rest on the Flight into Egypt."

- Private Apartments: These rooms, recently opened to the public, offer a glimpse into the family's daily life, showcasing period furnishings, personal artifacts, and additional works of art.

Visitor Tips

- The Palazzo Doria Pamphilj remains under the ownership of the Doria Pamphilj family. As of recent reports, Princess Gesine Doria Pamphilj, along with her children, lives in the private apartments of the palazzo. The family continues to manage and preserve the historic residence and its renowned art collection, ensuring that the legacy of the Doria Pamphilj lineage endures. This means some areas are off limits and guarded.

- Book tickets online in advance to guarantee entry, tickets do sell out.

- An engaging audio guide narrated by a member of the Doria Pamphilj family enriches the experience with personal insights into the collection and the family's history.

- Its central location makes it an ideal stop between other Baroque landmarks, such as the Trevi Fountain and the Pantheon.

The Galleria Doria Pamphilj provides a stunning example of Baroque opulence and artistic patronage, making it a must-see stop that bridges Rome's ancient heritage with its transformation into the Baroque cultural capital of Europe.

In Summary

Rome's architecture reveals a story of adaptation, resilience, and transformation. By examining these varied styles and structures—from the engineering feats of the Colosseum to the mathematical harmony of

Renaissance forms and the expressive dynamism of Baroque spaces—you gain insight into the cultural and artistic forces that have shaped Rome over the centuries. Each site on this tour tells a unique story, highlighting architectural principles that continue to inspire architects and artists worldwide.

Whether admiring the balance of the Tempietto or the grandeur of the Colosseum, this tour demonstrates how each architectural evolution has contributed to the living museum that is Rome. Your journey through these sites will offer a layered understanding of how Rome's architecture symbolizes not only a historical timeline but also the city's spirit and aspirations through the ages.

CHAPTER SIXTEEN

Holy Week and Easter during the Jubilee Year

La Settimana Santa

Holy Week and Easter

Pilgrims visiting Rome during Holy Week will have the rare opportunity to be in the city for Easter and the Jubilee. In addition, the Vatican is planning (but at the time of printing has not yet announced) several Jubilee-specific events tied to Holy Week. These include special gatherings and processions designed to deepen the sense of community and renewal among the millions of pilgrims expected to visit Rome.

Throughout Holy Week, major events like the Papal Mass on Easter Sunday and the Way of the Cross on Good Friday will be enhanced by the presence of indulgences, allowing pilgrims to gain spiritual benefits through penance, prayer, and charity

In April 2022, I embarked on what would become one of the most beautiful journeys of my life - spending Holy Week and Easter in Rome with my family. Words cannot capture the magic of those days. Rome seemed to glow with an otherworldly light as spring breathed new life into the city. The mornings greeted us with a crisp coolness that gradually yielded to the warm embrace of the Mediterranean sun. With each passing day, I felt more deeply connected to the rhythm of this ancient city, its cobblestone streets and timeless piazzas resonating with centuries of faith and tradition.

The experience of Holy Week and Easter in Rome transcends mere tourism - it's an immersion into living history, a chance to be part of something greater than oneself. From the solemn processions to the jubilant Easter Mass, every moment felt significant, every sight etched permanently in my memory.

I cannot recommend this experience highly enough. If you're considering when to visit Rome in 2025, let me assure you: Holy Week and Easter are, without a doubt, the most special times to be in this extraordinary city. It may well be the crowning jewel of all the celebrations Rome offers!

Join me as I guide you through the vibrant traditions and awe-inspiring events that make Easter in Rome an unparalleled experience. Let's embark on this journey together, and I'll share with you the moments that made my heart soar and my spirit sing.

Palm Sunday (Domenica delle Palme): Where History Meets Faith

As I stood in St. Peter's Square on Palm Sunday, the air thick with anticipation and the scent of olive branches, I felt the weight of centuries of tradition. This day, marking the beginning of Holy Week and commemorating Jesus Christ's triumphant entry into Jerusalem, was more powerful than I could have imagined.

Events in Rome

Mass at St. Peter's Square: Witnessing the Pope lead the special Mass was truly awe-inspiring. The blessing of palm and olive branches filled the air with a fresh, earthy aroma that seemed to connect us to the very soil of Italy. As the Pope processed through the square, carrying palms and re-enacting Jesus' entry into Jerusalem, I felt transported through time. The celebration of the Eucharist that followed was deeply moving. (Note: Tickets are required, and I recommend securing them well in advance.)

Traditional Processions: While the Vatican events were grand, I found equal beauty in the smaller processions throughout Rome. Walking through the ancient streets, joining locals carrying olive branches, I was struck by the intimacy of these neighborhood celebrations. Using olive branches instead of palm fronds was a delightful surprise, and I love the practical wisdom behind it. As a local explained to me, Italy's abundance of olive trees that need regular pruning makes this an ingenious, eco-friendly tradition. It felt like a beautiful blend of faith, sustainability, and Italian practicality.

A Tale of Palms, Popes, and Perseverance

During my visit, I was captivated by a story I'd read in R.A. Scotti's book "Basilica" (which I heartily recommend to anyone interested in the history of St. Peter's). It's a tale that exemplifies the spirit of innovation and determination that built the Vatican we see today.

In 1586, Pope Sixtus V faced a monumental challenge: moving a 320-ton Egyptian granite obelisk to the center of St. Peter's Square. This wasn't just any obelisk—it had stood witness to St. Peter's martyrdom and had resisted relocation for centuries. Even Michelangelo had deemed the task impossible.

The winning solution came from Domenico Fontana, whose ingenious plan involved an intricate system of ropes, pulleys, and manpower. On the day of the move, with 907 men and 145 horses assembled, Rome held its breath. The Pope had decreed silence on the pain of death, adding to the tension.

As the operation began, disaster loomed–the ropes started to smoke. In that critical moment, a sailor from Bordighera broke the silence, shouting, "Acqua alle funi!" (Water the ropes!). This simple suggestion saved the day.

In a beautiful twist of fate, the Pope granted Bordighera the perpetual honor of providing Easter palms to St. Peter's–a tradition that continues to this day. Fontana, for his part, was knighted and richly rewarded.

Standing in St. Peter's Square on Palm Sunday, holding my olive branch, I couldn't help but feel connected to this rich tapestry of history.

For those fortunate enough to tour the Tomb of St. Peter beneath the Basilica, keep an eye out for a square granite marking on the pavement outlined in white stone on the way to the Ufficio Scavi (the office where you meet your tour). This unassuming marker indicates where the obelisk originally stood–a silent testament to the incredible feat of engineering and the power of quick thinking that shaped this sacred space.

Holy Monday to Holy Wednesday

A Time for Reflection and Exploration

As I discovered during my visit, the early days of Holy Week offer a unique blend of spiritual reflection and opportunities for exploration. While the grand events were yet to come, these days held their own quiet power.

Holy Monday: Traditionally marking Jesus' cleansing of the temple, I found this day set a tone of purification and renewal. The city seemed to hold its breath, preparing for the days ahead.

Holy Tuesday: As we reflected on Jesus' predictions of betrayal, I was struck by the human drama at the heart of the Easter story. The weight of these ancient events felt palpable in Rome's historic streets.

Holy Wednesday: This day commemorates Judas' conspiracy with the Sanhedrin. The air of anticipation in Rome was almost tangible.

Personal Experiences and Tips:

During these quieter days, we took time to explore Rome more extensively. The walking tours included in this guide are based on my planning for this week. They will allow you to discover hidden gems and iconic sites alike. I'd recommend using these days to immerse yourself in Rome's rich history and culture - it adds depth to the Easter experience.

My cousin Susie and I took a treno veloce (fast train, 90 minutes) to Florence on Tuesday. While it meant missing some events in Rome, it offered a beautiful contrast and a chance to see how other parts of Italy prepare for Easter. If you can, I highly recommend a side trip. Just make sure you plan your return to Rome in time for the Holy Week events.

For those staying in Rome, consider visiting some of the less-known churches. I found that smaller, neighborhood churches often offered more intimate and deeply moving services during these days.

Remember to pace yourself - the most intense and crowded days are yet to come. Use this time to reflect, explore, and prepare yourself spiritually and physically for the profound experiences ahead.

As Holy Wednesday drew to a close, I felt a sense of anticipation building. The quiet reflection set the stage for upcoming events. I felt grateful for this preparation time.

Holy Thursday (Giovedì Santo)

The Last Supper Remembered

Holy Thursday marks a pivotal moment in the Easter story, commemorating the Last Supper when Jesus instituted the Eucharist and washed his disciples' feet. This day in Rome marked a palpable turning point, deepening the solemnity of the season.

From my experience, Rome remained relatively quiet from Palm Sunday through Holy Wednesday. However, on Holy Thursday, I noticed a significant increase in visitors. By Good Friday evening, during the Via Crucis, the city was bustling with pilgrims and tourists. If you're looking for a quieter Rome experience, I'd recommend arriving on the Saturday before Palm Sunday or on Palm Sunday itself. This timing allows you to settle in and explore the city more peacefully before the crowds arrive.

Key Events in Rome on Giovedi Santo:

- Chrism Mass

- Mass of the Lord's Supper

- Washing of the Feet (Lavanda dei Piedi)

- Adoration and Altars of Repose

Personal Reflection: Holy Thursday in Rome was a day of contrasts for me. The grandeur of the papal ceremonies juxtaposed with the intimate moments of prayer and reflection in smaller churches created a rich tapestry of experiences. I found the Giro delle Sette Chiese particularly meaningful. Walking through Rome's nighttime streets, moving from one sacred space to another, felt like a physical embodiment of a spiritual journey.

As the day ended, I sensed the city's atmosphere shifting. The growing crowds buzzed with anticipation. Holy Thursday set the stage for the profound events of Good Friday. I was privileged to be part of this ancient tradition in Rome.

Good Friday (Venerdì Santo): A Night of Solemn Reflection

Good Friday, the day Christians commemorate the Passion and Crucifixion of Jesus Christ, is marked by profound and moving events in Rome. The city takes on a somber yet deeply spiritual atmosphere as pilgrims and visitors gather to participate in centuries-old traditions.

Events in Rome:

Celebration of the Passion of the Lord: In the afternoon, the Pope presides over this solemn liturgy at St. Peter's Basilica. The service includes reading from the Gospel of John, venerating the Cross, and Holy Communion, creating a reverent atmosphere for the day.

Via Crucis (The Way of the Cross) at the Colosseum (highly recommended): The highlight of Good Friday in Rome is undoubtedly the Stations of the Cross, or Via Crucis, held at the Colosseum. This tradition, dating back to the 18th century, creates an unforgettable experience for all who attend.

As night falls, thousands of pilgrims, visitors, and religious figures gather around the illuminated Colosseum. The Pope leads the procession, guiding the faithful through the Stations of the Cross. Each station represents a moment in Christ's journey to Calvary, accompanied by prayers and hymns in multiple languages.

The Colosseum at moonrise when we entered for the Via Crucis, Way of the Cross with Pope Francis.

Personal Experience: The Via Crucis is truly a remarkable event. Under the moon and stars, beside the Colosseum, amidst fellow pilgrims, an indescribable unity and spiritual reflection emerge. The multi-lingual nature, with prayers and readings in various languages, emphasizes the universal nature of the observance. It was quite crowded outside the Colosseum where we attended but my understanding is Rome will start holding the event inside the Colosseum again this year. It changed because of COVID but it will change back.

Practical Information:

Tickets are not required, but attendees must pass through security checkpoints.

- Large bags are not permitted, so travel light. All bags are searched.

- Arrive early to secure a good viewing spot.

- Be prepared for a crowd—thousands attend this event each year.

- Comfortable shoes and warm clothing are recommended, as you'll be standing outdoors for several hours.

Broadcast: For those unable to attend in person, the Via Crucis is broadcast worldwide, making it one of the most widely watched Good Friday observances globally.

The combination of the ancient Colosseum—once a site of martyrdom—with the timeless story of Christ's sacrifice creates a deeply moving experience. With flickering torches, prayers in multiple languages, and faithful from all corners of the world, this Good Friday in Rome is a unique and memorable event. It's not just a religious ceremony, but a profound cultural experience that resonates with many, regardless of their faith background.

Holy Saturday (Sabato Santo)

A Day of Quiet Anticipation

Holy Saturday, also known as the Easter Vigil, is a day of quiet reflection and anticipation in the Christian calendar. It commemorates the day Jesus lay in the tomb before his resurrection. While less outwardly eventful than Good Friday or Easter Sunday, Holy Saturday holds deep spiritual significance and culminates in one of the most beautiful and symbolic services of the liturgical year.

Daytime in Rome and Beyond

While Rome becomes more filled with Easter visitors on Holy Saturday, my cousin Susie and I explored beyond the city limits. We ventured into the Castelli Romani, a cluster of picturesque towns in the Alban Hills southeast of Rome. We visited Frascati, Ariccia, Castel Gandolfo, Nemi, Genzano di Roma, Rocca di Papa and Grottaferrata. Luckily for us I had a friend from the area who knew their way around, had a car, and could transport us all over these beautiful villages.

Our day trip offered a unique glimpse into Italian Easter traditions outside the bustling capital. In these small towns, we witnessed a flurry of preparatory activity that contrasted with Rome's solemnity. Families lined up at local butcher shops, patiently waiting to collect their lamb for the traditional Easter Sunday feast. The streets were alive with residents running last-minute errands, their arms full of flowers, foods, and other holiday essentials.

In the smaller churches of the Castelli Romani, we observed the symbols and statues used for the Holy Week processions, including various statues of *Cristo Morto* (Christ after His removal from the Cross) in front of the altars. Each statue, a poignant representation of Jesus in repose, reflects the community's deep reverence and devotion, setting the stage for the solemn rituals of Holy Week.

This excursion provided a perfect balance to the intense spiritual experiences of the preceding days in Rome. While pilgrims in the city visited churches or engaged in quiet reflection on the events of Holy Week, our journey through the Castelli Romani allowed us to observe the more domestic side of Easter preparations. As the Church observes this solemn day, life continues. Families prepare to celebrate Easter joyfully in their homes.

For visitors to Rome during Holy Week, a day trip to the surrounding towns can offer a peaceful retreat and a chance to experience local culture away from the city's grand religious ceremonies. It provides a different perspective on how Italians observe this important religious holiday, blending spiritual tradition with family customs and culinary preparations.

The Easter Vigil (Vigilia Pasquale): The focal point of Holy Saturday is the Easter Vigil, which begins after sundown at St. Peter's Basilica, led by the Pope. This ancient service is rich in symbolism and tradition:

- Service of Light: The vigil begins in darkness, symbolizing the darkness of the tomb. The Paschal candle, representing the light of Christ, is lit from a new fire and carried into the darkened basilica. The light spreads as candles held by the faithful are lit from this single flame, gradually illuminating the entire church.

- Liturgy of the Word: This extended part of the service includes several readings from the Old and New Testaments, tracing salvation history from Creation to Resurrection. The Gloria is sung for the first time since Lent, often with bells ringing.

- Baptismal Liturgy: The Pope blesses the baptismal water, and the faithful renew their baptismal vows. New members are received into the Church through baptism during this service.

- Liturgy of the Eucharist: The vigil concludes with the celebration of the Eucharist, marking the joyous transition to Easter.

The Easter Vigil is considered the "mother of all vigils" in the Catholic tradition. It's a time of waiting and preparation, symbolizing the faithful's vigilant anticipation of Christ's return. The vigil's progression from darkness to light powerfully represents the movement from death to life central to the Easter story.

Practical Information for Visitors:

- While the main vigil is held at St. Peter's, many churches throughout Rome hold their own Easter Vigil services.

- The Vatican service is ticketed and extremely popular. Those wishing to attend should request tickets well in advance.

- The vigil typically lasts 3-4 hours, concluding around midnight with the ringing of bells and the illumination of church lights to celebrate the resurrection.

Even if not attending the service, visitors to Rome on Holy Saturday might notice the city's subdued atmosphere during the day, followed by a palpable sense of joy and celebration as Easter dawns.

While we spent this day exploring the beautiful Castelli Romani area, the Easter Vigil in Rome remains one of the most profound and moving liturgical experiences in the Christian world. It serves as a bridge between the solemnity of Good Friday and the exultation of Easter Sunday, encapsulating the heart of the Easter message in its rich symbolism and ancient traditions.

Easter Sunday (Pasqua)

A Celebration of Resurrection

Easter Sunday, celebrating the Resurrection of Jesus Christ, is the pinnacle of the Christian calendar. In Rome, this day is marked by grand celebrations and deeply moving spiritual experiences.

Easter Mass at St. Peter's Square: The Pope celebrates a solemn Mass in St. Peter's Square, attended by thousands of pilgrims and broadcast globally.

Personal Experience: Attending Easter Mass in St. Peter's Square is an unforgettable experience. As we took our seats near the obelisk, the atmosphere was electric with anticipation. The square was a sea of people, pilgrims, tourists, and locals alike, all gathered for this momentous occasion.

As the Mass began, a hush fell over the crowd. The spring sun shone brightly, casting a warm glow over the assembled faithful. What struck me most was the truly universal nature of the celebration. The Mass proceeded in multiple languages, Latin, English, Spanish, and others, each section seamlessly transitioning to the next. The multilingual approach beautifully represented the Church's global reach and believers' unity across the globe.

Mass in St. Peter's Square and façade of St. Peter's Basilica

Despite the thousands in attendance, there was an incredible sense of intimacy. The Pope's words, amplified across the square, seemed to reach everyone individually. The shared responses of the crowd, the collective moments of silence and reflection, all contributed to a profound sense of community and shared faith.

Urbi et Orbi Blessing: Following the Mass, the Pope delivers the "Urbi et Orbi" ("To the City and the World") blessing from the central loggia of St. Peter's Basilica. This special blessing, given on Easter and Christmas, often includes the Pope's reflections on global issues and prayers for peace and unity.

Pope in the Popemobile: In 2022, we were fortunate to get a closer view of Pope Francis thanks to his tour in the Popemobile after Mass and the Blessing. This added a personal touch to an already memorable day.

Practical Information for Attending Easter Mass:

Getting tickets for Easter Mass in St. Peter's Square can be challenging, but it is worthwhile. Here's what we learned:

- Tickets are distributed through the Prefecture of the Papal Household.

- Requests should be made well in advance (we started about 4 months ahead) by fax, including the date of the event, number of tickets needed, name or group name, mailing address, and contact information. My uncle Ted saved the day and found an international fax machine!

- Tickets can be collected in the morning prior to Mass.

- Arrive early to clear security (no large bags permitted) and secure good seats.

- Be prepared for crowds - even with assigned seating, standing crowds may fill the aisles.

Despite some initial frustrations with the crowds and seating arrangements, the experience of being present at this historic and spiritual event far outweighed any inconveniences. The atmosphere of joy, hope, and unity that permeates St. Peter's Square on Easter Sunday is truly one-of-a-kind, making it a profound highlight of any visit to Rome during Holy Week.

Chairs setup in Piazza San Pietro for Easter Mass

Mass in St. Peter's Square and façade of St. Peter's Basilica 2022. The morning was cool, but by the end of mass, our jackets were no longer needed.

Easter Monday (La Pasquetta)

A Day of Relaxation and Celebration

In Italy, Easter Monday, known as "Pasquetta" (Little Easter), is a public holiday that serves as a joyful continuation of the Easter celebrations. This day is traditionally dedicated to relaxation, outdoor activities, and social gatherings, offering a perfect balance to the solemnity of Holy Week.

Traditions and Activities in Rome:

Outdoor Gatherings: Romans typically spend this day with family and friends, enjoying picnics or day trips to the countryside. The city's parks and gardens, such as Villa Borghese or the Pincio Gardens, become lively hubs of activity.

Day Trips: Many locals take quick trips to nearby towns in the Castelli Romani or to the coast, embracing the spring weather and the opportunity to explore beyond the city.

Cultural Activities: While many businesses are closed, some museums and archaeological sites remain open, offering a chance for visitors to explore Rome's rich history without the usual crowds.

Culinary Traditions: Pasquetta is often associated with outdoor eating. Traditional foods might include leftover Easter dishes, frittatas, and various picnic-friendly items.

Special Masses: While less common than on Easter Sunday, some churches may hold special Masses or services for those seeking a spiritual component to their day.

For Visitors:

- Be aware that many shops and restaurants may be closed, so it's wise to plan.

- Public transportation usually runs on a holiday schedule.

- Popular picnic spots can get crowded, so arriving early is advisable if you plan to join in this tradition.

Easter Monday in Rome offers a unique glimpse into Italian culture, blending religious observance with joyful communal celebration. It's a day that encapsulates the Italian art of living well, emphasizing family, food, and enjoyment of the outdoors.

This relaxed and festive day serves as a fitting conclusion to Holy Week in Rome, a period that showcases the city's deep spiritual roots and rich cultural heritage. From the solemnity of Good Friday to the joy of Easter

Sunday and the relaxation of Pasquetta, Holy Week in Rome offers a profound and multifaceted experience for both locals and visitors, leaving lasting memories of this special time.

Important Churches in Rome that have Mass on Palm Sunday and Easter

In Rome, several important churches, besides St. Peter's Basilica, hold significant Palm Sunday and Easter Masses. These churches are often historic and are deeply connected to the religious and cultural heritage of the city. If you are unable to secure tickets for mass at St. Peter's Square here is a list of some of other options:

Basilica of St. John Lateran (San Giovanni in Laterano). The Basilica of St. John Lateran is the Pope's cathedral and the "Mother Church" of all Roman Catholic churches worldwide. It is one of the four major basilicas of Rome.

Basilica of St. Mary Major (Santa Maria Maggiore). One of the four major basilicas, St. Mary Major, is renowned for its stunning mosaics and is dedicated to the Virgin Mary.

Basilica of St. Paul Outside the Walls (San Paolo Fuori le Mura). Another of the four major basilicas, this church, is built over the tomb of St. Paul and is a key pilgrimage site.

Basilica of Santa Maria in Trastevere (St. Mary in Trastevere). In the Trastevere district, this basilica is one of the oldest churches in Rome dedicated to the Virgin Mary. It is celebrated for its beautiful mosaics and historical significance.

Basilica of Santa Maria sopra Minerva (St. Mary over Minerva's Roman Temple). Near the Pantheon, this is one of the few Gothic churches in Rome. It houses the tombs of St. Catherine of Siena and Fra Angelico.

Chiesa del Gesù (Church of the Gesù / Jesuit Order). The mother church of the Jesuit order, near Piazza Venezia. It is renowned for its Baroque architecture and its significance to the Society of Jesus.

Basilica of San Clemente (St. Clement). Famous for its layered history, this basilica is built over a fourth-century church, which itself is above a first-century Roman house.

Basilica of San Lorenzo fuori le Mura (St. Laurence outside the walls). One of the seven pilgrimage churches of Rome, it is dedicated to St. Lawrence and is one of the oldest basilicas in the city.

Basilica of Sant'Andrea della Valle (St. Andrew of the Valley). Near the Campo de' Fiori, this basilica is known for its gigantic dome and Baroque art.

Church of Sant'Ignazio di Loyola (St. Ignatius of Loyola). Another Jesuit church in Rome, renowned for its breathtaking ceiling frescoes and its connection to St. Ignatius of Loyola.

These churches, among others, offer a profound experience for worshippers and visitors during Palm Sunday, each with its own unique atmosphere and traditions. The city of Rome, with its rich history and deep spiritual roots, provides a deeply moving environment for observing this important day in the Christian calendar.

Easter Treats

Easter in Italy is celebrated with a variety of traditional foods that vary by region, but several dishes are commonly enjoyed across the country. These foods often reflect the season and have deep cultural and religious significance. Traditional Easter foods in Italy - an overview.

1. **Colomba Pasquale.** The "Colomba Pasquale," or Easter Dove, is a sweet, yeast bread similar to Panettone (which is popular at Christmas), but it is shaped like a dove or a cross. It's made with flour, eggs, sugar, and butter, and is typically studded with candied peel and topped with pearl sugar and almonds.

2. **Torta Pasqualina.** This savory pie originates from Liguria and is made with layers of thin pastry filled with a mixture of ricotta, spinach (or chard), Parmesan cheese, and often whole boiled eggs. The pie is said to symbolize the resurrection because of the eggs hidden inside.

3. **Agnello (Lamb).** Lamb is a traditional Easter dish in many parts of Italy, symbolizing purity and sacrifice. It is often roasted and served with potatoes and herbs like rosemary and garlic.

4. **Casatiello.** It is a savory, traditional bread from Naples, typically prepared during the Easter season. It's made from a rich dough that incorporates lard or butter, filled with a combination of cured meats like salami and ham, along with cheeses, such as pecorino or provolone.

5. **Pastiera Napoletana.** This is a traditional Neapolitan dessert made with a crust of shortcrust pastry filled with a mixture of ricotta, cooked wheat grains, eggs, sugar, and orange flower water.

It's often flavored with cinnamon and candied citrus peel.

6. **Uova di Pasqua** (Chocolate Easter Eggs). In modern times, chocolate Easter eggs have become a widespread tradition across Italy. Eggs in Italy are unlike those in America. The chocolate eggs can be as big as your purse or even your suitcase. They are hollow and they have toys inside, stuffed animals, almost like an Easter basket inside of an egg. They can cost 60, 100, even 500 euros. It is a unique tradition.

7. **Salami and eggs.** Especially common in Southern Italy, this dish is a simple yet hearty meal that involves cooking slices of salami and eggs together. It is often served at Easter Sunday breakfast.

These foods are central to the Italian Easter experience, symbolizing renewal, tradition, and community. Centuries-old dishes, prepared with love, still grace Italian homes today.

Casatiello

CHAPTER SEVENTEEN

Securing Tickets for Rome's Busiest Sites

Practical Advice for Maximizing your Time in Rome

I t pains me to see visitors to Rome wasting precious vacation time standing in long lines when there are tricks to skipping them!

Here is a list of the busiest sites and practical tips for getting tickets and planning your visit.

St. Peter's Basilica and the Vatican Museums

Advance Tickets: You can book tickets online in advance for the Vatican Museums and the Sistine Chapel, which will save you from waiting in the long lines. St. Peter's Basilica itself is free to enter, but you can book tours or a fast-track entry through various ticketing services.

Where to Book: Official Vatican Museums website (www.museivaticani.va) offers direct bookings.

Skip-the-Line Tickets: Available through the Vatican Museums website or other reputable vendors such as GetYourGuide or Viator. These services provide skip-the-line access and guided tours.

Practical Tip: Consider booking early morning or late afternoon time slots for quieter visits to the Vatican Museums and Sistine Chapel. Also, in the past this tour ends inside of St. Peter's Basilica so it is a "Skip the Line Entry" to the basilica but it won't be through the Holy Door.

Ancient Greek Sculpture in the Vatican Museum

The Borghese Gallery

The Borghese Gallery houses one of the most stunning collections of Renaissance and Baroque art in Rome, with masterpieces by Caravaggio, Bernini, and Raphael.

Advance Tickets: The Borghese Gallery has limited timed entry, and tickets must be purchased in advance as they often sell out weeks ahead.

Where to Book: Visit the official Borghese Gallery website (www.galleriaborghese.beniculturali.it) to secure your reservation.

Practical Tip: Tickets are issued in two-hour slots, so plan your visit accordingly. We booked a guided tour and it helped with time management because there is a lot of art to see in two hours. Most major tour operators offer these guided tours (Viator, TripAdvisor, Tours by Locals).

St. John Lateran (San Giovanni in Laterano)

As the Cathedral of Rome, St. John Lateran is one of the four major basilicas pilgrims will visit during the Jubilee. While entry is free, the basilica is expected to draw large crowds.

Advance Tickets: No tickets are required for general entry, but you can book special tours of the Lateran Palace or the Cloister for an enhanced visit.

I also recommend the audio guide the Basilica offers. It is a really great self-guided tour option.

Practical Tip: Aim to visit in the early morning or late afternoon to avoid the midday rush, especially during major liturgical events.

The Pantheon

One of the best-preserved monuments from ancient Rome, the Pantheon is a must-see. It is still an active church, and Mass is held regularly.

Advance Tickets: Entrance to the Pantheon is now ticketed, especially during high seasons. I wish I had a picture of the line 100 people deep every time we crossed through this piazza!

Where to Book: Tickets can be purchased on the Pantheon's official website (www.museumsrome.it), which offers timed entry to manage crowd flow.

*Catacombs of Rome

*See Catacombs of Rome Chapter for more detail.

The ancient Christian burial sites are a popular destination for pilgrims and history enthusiasts alike. The Catacombs of San Callisto and Catacombs of San Sebastiano are among the most visited.

Trevi Fountain and Spanish Steps

These iconic landmarks are must-see attractions, though they tend to be extremely crowded throughout the year. Visit early in the morning or late in the evening to experience these sites without the heavy crowds.

Guided Tours: Many of Rome's most famous sites offer guided tours, which can provide you with priority access and deeper insights into the history of each location. Pre-booking these tours can save you time and enhance your experience.

Colosseum, Roman Forum, and Palatine Hill

These iconic ancient Roman sites are some of the busiest tourist attractions in Rome. During the Jubilee, they will also attract pilgrims seeking to explore Rome's historical roots.

Advance Tickets: You REALLY need to purchase combination tickets for the Colosseum, Roman Forum, and Palatine Hill in advance. They sell out and it can be upsetting for people who have wanted to enter this historical site to be barred entry.

Tickets for the Colosseum can be purchased online through the official website, Parco Colosseo.

This site offers several types of tickets: standard entry, combination tickets (Colosseum + Roman Forum + Palatine Hill), and special access tickets for certain areas like the Arena Floor or the Underground.

Timed Entry: The Colosseum requires timed entry tickets, so be sure to reserve your spot ahead of time.

Practical Tip: Opt for early morning visits to avoid the midday rush. Booking a guided tour will also give you deeper insights into the history and significance of these sites.

As of October 18, 2023, all Colosseum tickets are required to be nominative, meaning each ticket must bear the name of the individual visitor. This measure aims to prevent unauthorized reselling and ensure that tickets are used by the intended individuals. Upon purchase, visitors must provide personal identification details, and identity checks are conducted at the entrance. Visitors are required to present a valid original ID matching the name on the ticket. If there's a discrepancy between the ticket and the ID, entry will be denied without a refund. The system allows for a one-time name change up to seven days before the visit date.

Also the "After Hours" and evening tours are very interesting and during the summer not has hot. (See Rome's Architectural Evolution Chapter forTo visit the Colosseum in Rome, you can purchase tickets through various methods, and here are the main options to consider:

Types of Tickets

- Basic Ticket: Includes access to the Colosseum, Roman Forum, and Palatine Hill. Tickets are usually valid for 24 hours from first use, allowing a single entry to each site.

- Full Experience Ticket: Adds access to the Arena Floor and the Underground (if available). You can book guided tours or audio guides for an extra fee.

- Special Tours: If you're interested in more exclusive areas, there are additional tickets for guided tours to the Underground, Belvedere, or the Arena, which are best booked well in advance.

Where to Buy Tickets

- Online: For convenience, buy tickets on the official website or from trusted resellers. Purchasing online means you'll get a QR code to use at the entrance, so you can skip the ticket line.

- Ticket Office: The Colosseum has an onsite ticket office, but be aware that lines can be long, especially during the high season. It's generally advised to go early in the morning if you choose this route.

- Via Tour Companies: Many companies offer tickets that include a guided tour. These are a good option if you're interested in historical commentary, but they typically come with an additional cost.

Entry Times and Logistics

The Colosseum usually opens at 8:30 a.m., with the last entry one hour before closing. It closes around sunset, but check the official site for seasonal hours.

The Colosseum allows only a limited number of visitors per time slot, so be sure to select a specific entry time when purchasing your tickets online.

Costs

Ticket prices vary, but here's an approximate guide:

- Standard Ticket: Around €16

- Reduced Ticket (for EU citizens between 18-25): Around €2

- Free Entry: For children under 18 and on the first Sunday of each month (however, the free entry often results in crowded conditions).

Special Tips & Colosseum Tours

Skip-the-Line Access: Opt for tickets with skip-the-line access if possible, as it can save you significant waiting time.

Avoid Scams: Use only the official Colosseum website or trusted vendors to avoid purchasing fake tickets.

Tour Operators Offer a Variety of Different Tours for the Colosseum.

Colosseum Arena Floor Tour

This tour offers exclusive access to the Arena Floor, allowing you to stand where gladiators once fought. It also includes visits to the Roman Forum and Palatine Hill, providing a comprehensive overview of ancient Rome.

Colosseum Underground Tour

Delve into the Colosseum's underground chambers, exploring the network of tunnels and rooms where gladiators and animals were prepared for the games. This tour often includes the Arena Floor and upper levels, offering a complete perspective of the monument.

Colosseum Night Tour

Experience the Colosseum illuminated after dark with a nighttime tour. These tours provide a unique ambiance and often include access to areas like the underground chambers, which are less crowded in the evening.

Colosseum and Ancient Rome Tour

This comprehensive tour covers the Colosseum, Roman Forum, and Palatine Hill. Guides provide in-depth historical context, making it ideal for first-time visitors interested in ancient Roman history.

Private Colosseum Tour

For a personalized experience, consider a private tour. These tours can be tailored to your interests and often include skip-the-line access, allowing you to explore at your own pace with a dedicated guide.

When selecting a tour, consider factors such as group size, duration, areas covered, and whether skip-the-line access is included. Booking in advance is recommended, especially during peak tourist seasons, to ensure availability and secure the best experience.

CHAPTER EIGHTEEN

Visiting the Catacombs of Rome

The Cities of the Dead

What Are Catacombs?

Catacombs are underground burial sites, often described as "underground cities," primarily used by early Christians in Rome to bury their dead during a time when the Church was still persecuted by the Roman Empire. These vast networks of tunnels and chambers were carved out of soft volcanic rock and feature niches for bodies (loculi), elaborate tombs for martyrs and saints, and stunning early Christian art, including frescoes, inscriptions, and sculptures.

Under ancient Roman law, burial sites had to be located outside the city limits for hygiene and public health reasons. Therefore, most of Rome's catacombs are found along major roads leading out of the city, such as the famous Appian Way. Burial within the city was strictly forbidden, and both pagans and Christians adhered to this regulation.

Early Christians used these catacombs not only for burial but also for secret worship during times of persecution. These burial sites offered a secluded place for the Christian community to gather in peace and honor their dead. The catacombs served as a symbolic expression of the Christian belief in resurrection and eternal life. For early Christians, burying their loved ones in these subterranean chambers was a testament to their faith in salvation through Christ.

Visiting the catacombs today provides a powerful connection to this early period of Christian history, offering insight into their devotion, artistry, and resilience in the face of adversity.

Why Visit One the Seven Catacombs?

Visiting the catacombs offers a deeply moving and educational experience for those interested in early Christian history, Roman culture, and art. Here's why a visit to these ancient burial sites is a must:

Step Back in Time to Early Christianity: The catacombs of Rome provide a rare glimpse into the early Christian community during its formative years. By walking through these ancient tunnels, visitors can connect with the very beginnings of Christian worship and burial practices. The tombs of martyrs, the inscriptions of hope and faith, and the relics of saints make these visits both spiritual and historical journeys.

Discover Beautiful Early Christian Art: Despite their somber purpose, the catacombs are adorned with some of the oldest Christian art in existence. You'll find frescoes that depict biblical scenes, ancient symbols of Christianity like the fish (Ichthys), and images of saints and martyrs. These artworks offer insight into how early Christians visualized their faith, and many pieces are astonishingly well-preserved despite being centuries old.

Explore Roman History from a Unique Perspective: The catacombs were not only burial places but also a reflection of the social and religious changes in Rome. The rise of Christianity, the influence of Roman customs on early Christian burial practices, and the perseverance of the faithful through persecution all unfold within these labyrinthine spaces. You'll gain an understanding of Rome's transformation from a pagan empire to a Christian one.

A Quiet, Reflective Escape: In contrast to the bustling streets of modern Rome, the catacombs offer a peaceful and introspective atmosphere. It's a space for quiet reflection, where visitors can contemplate the resilience of early Christians and the endurance of faith across centuries. The cool, dim tunnels also provide a unique experience that contrasts with the grandeur of Rome's more famous above-ground monuments.

A Fascinating Exploration of Roman Engineering: The sheer scale of the catacombs is a testament to Roman engineering. Spanning miles underground, these burial sites reveal the ingenuity of ancient Romans in creating functional, hidden spaces that could accommodate thousands of burials over centuries.

Visiting the catacombs is more than just seeing burial chambers—it's stepping into the hidden layers of Rome's religious and cultural history. Whether you are a pilgrim, history enthusiast, or simply curious about this ancient practice, the catacombs offer a moving and unforgettable experience that deepens your understanding of the Eternal City's spiritual and historical legacy.

While some catacombs have websites for ticket bookings, others may require on-site purchasing or third-party tour arrangements.

Catacombs of San Callisto (Catacombe di San Callisto)

Location: Via Appia Antica

Why Visit: Among the largest and most significant Christian burial sites in Rome, the Catacombs of San Callisto are famous for the Crypt of the Popes. They also contain remarkable early Christian frescoes and inscriptions.

Booking Information: You can purchase tickets on-site or book through official tours.

Website: San Callisto Catacombs Official Site–Offers online ticket purchases and information about guided tours. https://www.catacombesancallisto.it/en/index.php

Catacombs of San Sebastiano (Catacombe di San Sebastiano)

Location: Via Appia Antica

Why Visit: The resting place of Saint Sebastian, the catacombs are known for their well-preserved galleries and tombs. You'll also see frescoes and inscriptions from the early Christian era.

Booking Information: Tickets are sold on-site, but it's recommended to check availability in advance through official websites or tour providers.

Website: https://www.catacombe.org/

Catacombs of Domitilla (Catacombe di Domitilla)

Location: Via delle Sette Chiese

Why Visit: The largest of Rome's catacombs, Domitilla offers a journey through 17 kilometers of underground tunnels. A highlight is the underground basilica and the tombs of Saints Nereus and Achilleus.

Booking Information: Tickets are available on-site, or you can book through third-party tour companies.

Website: Catacombs of Domitilla. Provides information on visiting hours and tour bookings.

https://www.catacombedomitilla.it/en

Catacombs of Priscilla (Catacombe di Priscilla)

Location: Via Salaria

Why Visit: The Catacombs of Priscilla are known for their ancient Christian frescoes, including one of the earliest images of the Virgin Mary. They are also the burial place of many early Christian martyrs.

Booking Information: You can book tours directly through their website or visit without a reservation, although it's recommended to book during busy times.

Website: Catacombs of Priscilla – Online booking available for guided tours. https://catacombepriscilla.com/en/home-en/

Catacombs of St. Agnes (Catacombe di Sant'Agnese)

Location: Via Nomentana

Why Visit: Named after Saint Agnes, these catacombs are significant for their association with this early Christian martyr. They are near the Basilica of St. Agnes Outside the Walls, another important pilgrimage site.

Booking Information: Tickets are usually available on-site. Some tours include visits to both the catacombs and the basilica.

Website: https://www.santagnese.net/site/catacombs-mausoleum/

Catacombs of Marcellinus and Peter (Catacombe dei Santi Marcellino e Pietro)

Location: Via Casilina

Why Visit: These catacombs, dedicated to two Roman martyrs, are known for their beautiful frescoes. Though smaller, they offer an intimate exploration of early Christian burial practices.

Booking Information: Tours are often arranged through third-party tour operators.

Website: There is no direct website for these catacombs, but tours can be arranged through various Rome tour companies.

Catacombs of St. Paul (Catacombe di San Paolo)

Location: Near St. Paul Outside the Walls on Via Ostiense

Why Visit: These catacombs are historically significant due to their proximity to the Basilica of St. Paul Outside the Walls, one of Rome's four major basilicas. The catacombs were used to bury early Christians, and St. Paul was once buried here before being moved to the basilica.

Booking Information: These catacombs are generally not open to the public but may be for special events of the Jubilee year. Tours of the nearby basilica can be booked via the basilica's official site.

Website: Basilica of St. Paul Outside the Walls – For information on the basilica and the area around the catacombs.

CHAPTER NINETEEN

Shopping in Rome

From Historic Markets to High End Designer Brands

Rome's shopping scene reflects its rich cultural heritage, offering everything from historic luxury boutiques to vibrant local markets. Like the city itself, each shopping district tells a unique story, blending history, culture, and modern commerce into an unforgettable experience.

The Fashion Triangle

At the heart of Rome's luxury shopping lies a historic triangle of streets, each with its own distinct character. The most famous, Via dei Condotti, has been the epicenter of Italian haute couture since the 18th century. Running from the iconic Spanish Steps to Via del Corso, this elegant street was originally named for the ancient conduits that carried water to the Baths of Agrippa. Today, it hosts flagship stores of the world's most prestigious fashion houses, including the historic Bulgari shop (established 1905) and flagship stores of Gucci, Prada, Valentino, and Louis Vuitton.

For a taste of history while shopping, stop at the famous Caffè Greco at number 86. Established in 1760, this historic café once welcomed literary giants like Goethe, Byron, and Keats. To experience the best service and avoid crowds, plan your shopping excursion for early morning when shops open at 10:00 AM.

Complementing Via dei Condotti are two other notable shopping streets. Via del Corso, stretching 1.5 kilometers from Piazza Venezia to Piazza del Popolo, offers a mix of international brands and Italian fashion housed in historic palazzos. The street's name recalls its history as a horse racing venue during Carnival celebrations until the late 19th century. Today, shoppers can find everything from global retailers like Zara and H&M to Italian brands like OVS and Imperial.

The third side of this shopping triangle, Via del Babuino, takes its name from a distinctive statue of a sileno (often mistaken for a baboon) adorning a street fountain. Since the 17th century, this elegant thoroughfare has been known for its art galleries, antique shops, and luxury vintage boutiques, all housed within historic palazzi.

Rome's Historic Markets

For a more authentic Roman shopping experience, the city's historic markets offer vibrant alternatives to designer boutiques. Campo de' Fiori, active since 1869, transforms each morning into a colorful display of fresh produce, flowers, and local specialties. The market runs Monday through Saturday until 2:00 PM, offering everything from traditional Roman spice mixes to artisanal breads. The square's central statue of Giordano Bruno reminds visitors of its somber history as a site of public executions.

Sunday mornings bring the sprawling Porta Portese Flea Market to life in Trastevere. Established after World War II, this kilometer-long market features antiques, vintage clothing, books, and artisanal crafts. Early birds get the best finds, so arrive before 8:00 AM and bring cash for negotiating.

For a modern twist on market culture, Mercati Monti showcases emerging designers and vintage collectors in one of Rome's oldest neighborhoods. Open weekends, this urban market has become a hub for independent fashion designers, vintage curators, and local artists.

Specialty Shopping

Rome excels in specialty shops, particularly for books and religious items. English-language book lovers should visit the Almost Corner Bookshop in Trastevere or the atmospheric Open Door Bookshop. For religious items, the streets near the Vatican, particularly Via dei Cestari, host historic shops like Barbiconi, which has supplied vestments to the Vatican since 1920.

Eataly Roma: A Modern Food Emporium

No shopping guide to Rome would be complete without mentioning Eataly Roma, near the Ostiense train station. This modern food emporium spans multiple floors, offering markets, restaurants, and cooking classes. Its fine dining establishments–Terra, Pizza & Cucina, and Il Mare–require reservations, especially for weekend dinners. With 23 eating venues, fresh market sections, and an extensive wine cellar housing over 5,000 labels, Eataly represents Rome's evolution into a modern culinary destination.

Shopping Hours and Tips

Most Rome shops open around 10:00 AM and close at 8:00 PM, with some observing the traditional riposo (afternoon break) between 1:00-4:00 PM. While credit cards are widely accepted in boutiques and department stores, local markets typically require cash. Remember that many shops close on Sundays, except for markets like Porta Portese and tourist areas around major attractions.

Whether you're seeking haute couture, antique treasures, or local specialties, Rome's diverse shopping scene offers something for every taste and budget. Each purchase becomes part of the city's continuing story, connecting modern shoppers to centuries of Roman commerce and culture.

CHAPTER TWENTY

Rome's Artistic Titans

Unveiling the Masterpieces of Michaelangelo, Caravaggio, and Bernini

R ome's artistic legacy was profoundly shaped by three revolutionary artists: Michelangelo Buonarroti (1475-1564), Gian Lorenzo Bernini (1598-1680), and Michelangelo Merisi da Caravaggio (1571-1610). Their works can be found throughout the city, from famous basilicas to hidden church chapels.

Michelangelo in Rome

Michelangelo Buonarroti (1475-1564) first arrived in Rome in 1496 as an ambitious 21-year-old sculptor, already showing the genius that would revolutionize Western art. Unlike his contemporaries who specialized in one medium, Michelangelo mastered sculpture, painting, and architecture, though he always considered himself primarily a sculptor, famously saying that painting the Sistine Chapel was "not my art." His volatile relationship with powerful patrons, especially Pope Julius II, shaped both his career and Rome's artistic landscape.

Operating without a traditional workshop and often working in solitude, Michelangelo's perfectionism and intense working methods set him apart from other Renaissance masters. He believed his sculptures were already complete within the marble, and his job was simply to chip away the excess stone to reveal them. This philosophy, combined with his unparalleled technical skill and deep understanding of human anatomy, resulted in works of unprecedented power and grace.

Throughout his 75-year career, Rome became both his greatest challenge and his greatest triumph. Though he maintained strong ties to his native Florence, it was in Rome where he created his most iconic works. His influence was so profound that after his death at 88, artists spoke of "la terribilità" - the terrifying power of Michelangelo's genius that both inspired and intimidated successive generations.

Pietà (1498-1499)

Location: St. Peter's Basilica, First Chapel on right after entrance

Michelangelo carved this masterpiece from a single block of Carrara marble when he was just 24 years old. It's the only work he ever signed, reportedly after overhearing visitors attribute it to another sculptor. The signature can be found across Mary's chest: MICHAELA[N]GELUS BONAROTUS FLORENTIN[US] FACIEBA[T] ("Michelangelo Buonarroti, Florentine, made this").

The piece revolutionized the pietà tradition by depicting a youthful Mary holding her deceased son. When questioned about Mary's youth, Michelangelo defended his choice, explaining that virginal purity preserves youth's beauty. The technical mastery is evident in multiple details:

Christ's muscles remain anatomically perfect while appearing lifeless; Mary's drapery flows naturally; her face shows restrained grief rather than excessive emotion.

In 1972, the sculpture was damaged by Laszlo Toth, who attacked it with a hammer. After careful restoration, it was protected behind bulletproof glass.

Visiting Details:

- Best viewed early morning before crowds gather.

- Note the contrasting textures: polished skin versus rough fabric.

- Look for the "M" fold in Mary's left hand, a signature Michelangelo detail.

Sistine Chapel Ceiling (1508-1512)

Location: Vatican Museums, Viale Vaticano

Initially reluctant to accept the commission, Michelangelo considered himself primarily a sculptor. Pope Julius II, however, insisted, leading to four years of physical hardship and artistic triumph. Despite popular belief, Michelangelo did not paint lying down but worked standing on scaffolding, craning his neck upward. He wrote a poem about his physical suffering during the project, describing paint dripping on his face and his neck permanently craned backward.

The ceiling's complex program includes nine scenes from Genesis, seven prophets, five sibyls, and numerous other figures. The famous Creation of Adam represents just one panel of this massive undertaking. Michelangelo worked from back to front, and his style developed to become larger and bolder as he realized viewers would see the work from 60 feet below.

Recent restoration (1980-1994) removed centuries of candle soot and previous restorations, revealing bright colors that surprised many art historians. Debate continues about whether the cleaning was too aggressive.

Visiting Details:

- Book first entrance or last two hours for fewer crowds.

- Bring small binoculars for detail viewing.

- Notice how figures become larger and bolder toward the entrance.

The Last Judgment (1536-1541)

Location: Sistine Chapel, Vatican Museums, Viale Vaticano

Commissioned by Pope Paul III, this massive fresco on the Sistine Chapel's altar wall marked Michelangelo's return to painting after 24 years. Unlike the ceiling's bright optimism, this work reflects the artist's darker vision and the religious tensions of the Reformation era. Christ appears as an imposing judge rather than a gentle savior, while boats ferry souls to their eternal destinations.

The work proved immediately controversial. Church officials objected to the nudity, leading to the "Fig Leaf Campaign" where Daniele da Volterra was hired to paint draperies over the nude figures. Michelangelo included his self-portrait in the flayed skin held by St. Bartholomew, possibly reflecting his own feelings about the project's toll.

Biagio da Cesena, the papal master of ceremonies who criticized the nudity, found himself portrayed in Hell as Minos with donkey ears and a snake biting his crotch. When he complained to the Pope, the pontiff reportedly joked that his jurisdiction didn't extend to Hell, so the portrait would have to remain.

Viewing Details:

- View from left to right to follow narrative sequence.

- Look for self-portrait in flayed skin held by St. Bartholomew.

- Notice contrast between saved souls' upward spiral and damned souls' downward plunge.

- The original colors were revealed in 1994 restoration.

Moses (1513-1515)

Location: San Pietro in Vincoli, (Saint Peter in Chains), Piazza di San Pietro in Vincoli, 4A

Originally intended as part of a magnificent 40-statue tomb for Pope Julius II, the Moses became one of Michelangelo's most powerful and controversial works. The sculptor spent over 40 years wrestling with the tomb project, though it was never completed to his original design. The Moses was meant to be one of six colossal figures overlooking the Pope's sarcophagus.

The marble statue depicts Moses after descending from Mount Sinai with the Ten Commandments, catching the Israelites worshipping the Golden Calf.

Michelangelo captured the precise moment when Moses, filled with righteous anger, is about to rise from his seat and shatter the tablets. The tension is visible in every detail, from the twisted pose of the torso to the rippling muscles beneath the robe.

Moses by Michaelangelo

The famous "horns" on Moses's head resulted from a mistranslation of the Hebrew text describing Moses's face as "radiating light" or "cornuta" (horned) in the Latin Vulgate Bible. Rather than a mistake, Michelangelo transformed this translation into a powerful artistic symbol of divine inspiration.

Michelangelo's Moses is celebrated for its revolutionary portrayal of psychological intensity, capturing the complex emotions of the biblical figure in a moment of righteous anger. The sculpture exemplifies Michelangelo's masterful carving technique, particularly visible in the intricate details of Moses's beard and the drapery of his robe.

This work significantly influenced the dramatic expression seen in later Baroque sculpture, inspiring artists to bring a similar vitality to their figures. Michelangelo himself regarded Moses as one of his most lifelike works, a testament to his skill in imbuing marble with dynamic energy and realism.

According to legend, upon completing the statue, Michelangelo struck Moses's knee with his hammer and commanded, "Now speak!" The mark is said to still be visible today.

Michelangelo's Moses within the funerary
monument of the Tomb of Pope Julius II

Visiting Details:

- Best viewed in morning light (church opens at 8:00)

- Right-hand side of the church's main altar

- Coins needed for illumination

- Notable detail: visible veins in Moses's left arm holding the tablets

The Chains of St Peter

- This church also holds the miraculous chains that bound St. Peter so it is worth a visit.

The Risen Christ (1519-1521)

Location: Santa Maria sopra Minerva, Piazza della Minerva, 42

This marble statue represents a unique portrayal of Christ, shown nude (now partially draped) embracing the cross. The work was commissioned by patrician Metello Vari, who specifically requested a "standing Christ holding the cross." Michelangelo's first version had a dark vein running through Christ's face, causing him to abandon it and start anew.

The final version shows extraordinary technical skill in carving Christ's muscles and the cross from a single block of marble. The figure's expression conveys both acceptance and determination, while the contrapposto pose recalls classical sculpture. Though assistants completed some details, the main figure unmistakably shows Michelangelo's mastery.

Visiting Details:

- Located to the left of the main altar

- Best viewed in morning light

- Note the contrast between polished skin and rougher cross

- Original bronze decorations added later by others

The Light and Shadow of Caravaggio in Rome

Michelangelo Merisi da Caravaggio (1571-1610) arrived in Rome in 1592 as a penniless young artist and within a decade revolutionized the history of painting. Unlike Michelangelo or Bernini, who enjoyed long careers and papal patronage, Caravaggio blazed through Rome like a comet - brilliant, revolutionary, and ultimately destructive. His innovations in chiaroscuro (the dramatic use of light and shadow) and unflinching realism changed art forever.

Known for his volatile temperament as much as his artistic genius, Caravaggio brought a raw authenticity to religious subjects by using ordinary people as models and setting sacred scenes in contemporary environments. His Roman period ended abruptly in 1606 when he fled the city after killing a man during a sword fight over a game of tennis. Despite his brief time in Rome, he left an extraordinary legacy of works that would influence artists for centuries.

Working without preparatory drawings, Caravaggio painted directly on canvas, often using the dark backgrounds that would become his trademark. He repeatedly found himself in trouble with religious authorities for using prostitutes and street people as models for saints and the Virgin Mary, yet his powerful depictions of spiritual moments attracted important patrons who protected him until his final, fatal controversy.

The Calling of Saint Matthew (1599-1600)

Location: Contarelli Chapel, San Luigi dei Francesi, Via di Santa Giovanna d'Arco 5

One of Caravaggio's most celebrated works shows the moment Christ calls Matthew, a tax collector, to discipleship. The scene takes place in a contemporary Roman tavern rather than a biblical setting. Christ's hand echoes God's hand from Michelangelo's Creation of Adam, while a beam of light dramatizes the divine moment of calling.

The identity of Matthew in the painting remains debated - is he the bearded man pointing to himself, or the young man counting money? This ambiguity adds to the work's power. Caravaggio's use of contemporary dress and setting caused controversy but made the spiritual moment immediately accessible to viewers.

The dramatic lighting creates a theatrical effect while serving theological purposes - the light of Christ's grace penetrates the dark world of the tax collector's den. Recent restoration has revealed more detail in the darker portions while confirming Caravaggio's innovative technique of incising lines directly into wet paint.

Visiting Details:

- Bring coins for chapel lighting.

- Stand back to see how light beam unifies composition.

- Note modern clothing and realistic faces across the three paintings.

The Martyrdom of Saint Matthew (1599-1600)

Location: Contarelli Chapel, San Luigi dei Francesi, Via di Santa Giovanna d'Arco 5

Companion to The Calling of Saint Matthew, this dramatic scene captures the violent moment of the saint's martyrdom. Caravaggio places the viewer directly in front of the attack, with the assassin's half-naked body forming a dramatic diagonal across the canvas. The artist included himself in the crowd of onlookers, his face emerging from the darkness as a witness to the martyrdom.

The painting demonstrates Caravaggio's revolutionary approach to religious art - the scene feels like a contemporary street murder rather than a distant historical event. The angel offering the palm of martyrdom to Matthew appears to float naturally into the space rather than descend on artificial clouds, while the architectural setting suggests a contemporary Roman baptistery.

Technical analysis reveals many pentimenti (changes), particularly in the position of the angel, showing how Caravaggio composed directly on canvas without preparatory drawings. The work's restoration in the 1960s removed centuries of candle soot, revealing the painting's original dramatic contrasts.

This painting forms a triptych with Calling and Saint Matthew and Angel. You should view all three works to understand narrative sequence. Be sure to look for Caravaggio's self-portrait in background.

Madonna of the Palafrenieri (1605-1606)

Location: Galleria Borghese, Piazzale Scipione Borghese 5

Originally painted for St. Peter's Basilica but rejected within days of installation, this work found a home in the Borghese collection. The painting shows Mary and Saint Anne (Mary's mother) teaching the Christ child to crush a serpent (representing sin), but Caravaggio's treatment was too unconventional for church authorities.

The artist's decision to show Mary as a young woman in contemporary dress, with Saint Anne as an elderly grandmother figure, and the child as a truly natural toddler, challenged religious artistic conventions. The snake is portrayed with shocking realism, likely painted from a dead specimen.

Recent restoration has revealed Caravaggio's complex layering technique, showing how he built up shadows gradually rather than painting them directly. The work's rejection from St. Peter's marks a turning point in Caravaggio's relationship with religious patrons.

Visiting Details:

- Requires advance booking at Borghese Gallery. Limited to 2-hour visiting slots.

- You should compare with other rejected religious works in collection at the Borghese.

The Conversion of Saint Paul (1601)

Location: Cerasi Chapel, Santa Maria del Popolo, Piazza del Popolo 12

Controversial from its unveiling, this painting shows Paul's conversion as an intimate, ground-level scene dominated by a horse's posterior rather than heavenly drama. The first version was rejected, forcing Caravaggio to paint this second version. The horse's bottom prominently positioned above the fallen saint scandalized viewers but emphasized Paul's humbling encounter with divine grace.

The painting uses Caravaggio's signature dramatic lighting to focus attention on Paul's vulnerable position. The saint's armor reflects light while his closed eyes suggest internal illumination. The groom holding the horse remains unaware of the miraculous event, highlighting the personal nature of divine revelation.

Technical analysis has revealed no preliminary drawings. Caravaggio painted directly on the canvas, adjusting positions as he worked. The horse's careful anatomical detail suggests he studied in Roman stables, consistent with his practice of painting from life.

Visiting Details:

- Chapel is small; patience needed during crowds.

- Compare with companion piece of Peter's crucifixion.

Bernini & Baroque Rome

Gian Lorenzo Bernini (1598-1680) transformed Rome more than any artist before or since. The son of successful Mannerist sculptor Pietro Bernini, young Gian Lorenzo was a child prodigy who began working in his father's studio at an extraordinary early age. Pope Paul V, after seeing the young Bernini's talent, prophetically proclaimed, "This child will be the Michelangelo of his age."

Unlike many artists who experienced their greatest achievements posthumously, Bernini was celebrated during his lifetime, becoming the preferred artist of eight popes. His father's position in Rome and early training provided crucial foundations, but Gian Lorenzo quickly surpassed his teacher. By his early twenties, he was already receiving major commissions and would go on to define the Baroque style through his dynamic sculptures and architectural projects.

Operating a large workshop from his studio near Piazza di Spagna, Bernini controlled most major artistic projects in Rome for over half a century. Unlike Michelangelo, who often worked in solitude, Bernini embraced the role of artistic director, orchestrating teams of artists and craftsmen to realize his grand visions. His works not only decorated Rome but fundamentally changed how people experienced art, creating theatrical environments that engaged viewers emotionally and spiritually.

Colonnade of St. Peter's Square (1656-1667)

Location: Piazza San Pietro, Vatican City

One of Bernini's greatest architectural achievements, the colonnade at Piazza San Pietro was commissioned by Pope Alexander VII to create an inviting, symbolic entrance to St. Peter's Basilica. Comprising 284 Doric columns arranged in a grand elliptical shape, the colonnade forms two semicircular arms that reach out to embrace visitors, symbolizing the welcoming arms of the Church.

Bernini masterfully designed the colonnade to enhance the spatial and spiritual experience, merging architecture with symbolism. Standing within one of two specific spots marked on the ground, a viewer sees all the columns line up perfectly—a testament to Bernini's architectural genius. Atop the colonnade, statues of 140 saints gaze down on the square, emphasizing the connection between heaven and earth.

Bernini's spectacular colonnade and St. Peter's Square

Baldacchino / Baldachin (1624-1633)

Location: St. Peter's Basilica, Vatican City

Standing 29 meters high, this massive bronze canopy marks the papal altar and St. Peter's tomb beneath. Pope Urban VIII commissioned this architectural sculpture, melting bronze from the Pantheon's portico (leading to the saying "What the barbarians didn't do, the Barberini did"). The spiraling columns were inspired by the ancient twisted columns that supposedly came from Solomon's temple in Jerusalem.

The Baldachin revolutionized church decoration by combining architecture and sculpture in unprecedented ways. The columns appear to be draped in fabric, defying the material's rigidity. Bernini incorporated the Barberini family's heraldic bees crawling up the columns, while olive and laurel branches suggest peace and victory.

During construction, critics claimed the structure would be impossible to cast and would collapse. Bernini proved them wrong through innovative casting techniques and engineering. The total cost was enormous: 200,000 Roman scudi, equivalent to millions today.

Visiting Details:

- Walk completely around to see all sculptural details.

- Look for the Barberini bees ascending the columns.

- Notice how the canopy frames the Cathedra Petri beyond.

Apollo and Daphne (1622-1625)

Location: Borghese Gallery, Piazzale Scipione Borghese 5

Considered one of Bernini's most remarkable achievements, this marble group captures the exact moment of Daphne's transformation into a laurel tree as she flees Apollo. The technical virtuosity is astounding - leaves appear to sprout from fingers, bark peels from flesh, and hair transforms into foliage, all carved from a single block of marble.

Cardinal Scipione Borghese commissioned the work, though its pagan subject required justification in Counter-Reformation Rome. A moral inscription was added: those pursuing earthly pleasures are left embracing mere trees. The sculpture shows Bernini's unmatched ability to transform solid marble into seemingly fluid forms.

Apollo and Daphne in the Galleria Borghese

Recent restoration revealed traces of original gold leaf on the leaves and subtle coloring that would have enhanced the transformation effect. The work influenced sculptors for centuries, though few could match its technical brilliance.

Fountain of the Four Rivers (1648-1651)

Location: Piazza Navona, Central Rome

This masterpiece represents the four major rivers known to Renaissance geography: the Nile (Africa), Ganges (Asia), Danube (Europe), and Rio de la Plata (Americas). The fountain supports an ancient Egyptian obelisk, creating a stunning vertical thrust in the piazza's center.

Popular legend claims Bernini designed the Rio de la Plata figure shielding his eyes in horror from the nearby church façade by his rival Borromini. However, the fountain was completed before the church's façade, debunking this myth. Each river god exhibits distinct characteristics: the Nile's head is veiled (as its source was then unknown), while the Rio de la Plata sits amid coins representing New World wealth.

The technical achievement is remarkable - the massive travertine blocks appear weightless, with the obelisk seemingly supported by open space. The fountain functions as both engineering marvel and theatrical performance, with water animating the sculptural groups.

Visiting Details:

- Piazza Navona is quietest around 7am. Great time for photographs.

- Listen for the different water sounds, deliberately engineered.

- Walk completely around to identify each river's symbols. Notice how figures interact with negative space.

Ecstasy of Saint Teresa (1647-1652)

Location: Cornaro Chapel, Santa Maria della Vittoria, Via XX Settembre 17

Perhaps Bernini's most controversial masterpiece, this sculptural group depicts Saint Teresa of Ávila's vision of being pierced by an angel's golden arrow. Bernini translated Teresa's mystical writing into visual form, showing the saint in spiritual ecstasy upon a cloud while a smiling angel prepares to pierce her heart.

The work exemplifies Baroque integration of arts - sculpture, architecture, and light work together to create a theatrical experience. Hidden windows cast natural light on the marble group, while gilded bronze rays enhance the supernatural effect.

Contemporary critics noted the sensual nature of Teresa's expression, though Bernini defended it as accurate to her own description. The sculpture represents the height of Baroque attempts to make spiritual experiences tangible through art.

CHAPTER TWENTY-ONE

Volunteering in the Spirit of the Jubilee

Hands of Grace

The Jubilee Year offers not only a spiritual experience but also the opportunity for individuals to become actively involved in helping the millions of pilgrims who will travel to Rome. By volunteering, participants engage more personally, help those in need, and ensure the smooth running of a significant Catholic celebration.

How to Become a Volunteer

If you are over 18 and want to help during the Jubilee, this is your chance to make a difference! Volunteers can offer their time for one or more weeks or take part in specific Jubilee events. Volunteers will assist pilgrims on their journeys to the Holy Doors of the four Papal Basilicas, provide information, and offer general assistance along the designated pilgrimage routes.

Steps to Become a Volunteer

Register: Sign up through the official Jubilee website (www.iubilaeum2025.va) or the Iubilaeum25 app. Once registered, you will receive access to a personal area where you can manage your volunteer availability.

Upload required Documents:

- A valid identification document (a clear and legible scan).

- A passport-style photograph (recent color, with a neutral background).

- A letter of recommendation from your parish priest or

- ecclesial leader confirming your active participation in the Catholic faith (a template is available for download).

Provide Availability: Volunteers can select specific weeks of availability (Saturday to Saturday) or sign up for particular Jubilee events. Please confirm availability before assignment. Volunteers may withdraw up to seven days before service starts.

Receive Confirmation: The Jubilee's Organizational Secretariat will review applications and confirm the acceptance of volunteers based on logistical needs. Volunteers will be notified of their assignments accordingly.

Volunteers play a vital role in ensuring the success of the Jubilee and acting as witnesses to the spirit of the Holy Year.

CHAPTER TWENTY-TWO

Calendar of Events Jubilee 2025

Jubilee Year at a Glance and General Information

Introduction to the Jubilee Calendar of Events

The Jubilee Year promises to be an extraordinary time in Rome, filled with sacred rituals, processions, celebrations, and spiritual milestones that have been observed for centuries. For those embarking on this unique pilgrimage, understanding the key events throughout the year will enhance your experience, allowing you to fully immerse yourself in the spiritual and cultural atmosphere of the Eternal City.

From the majestic opening of the Holy Doors to the special Masses held in Rome's most important basilicas, each event deepens the sense of renewal and grace that the Jubilee year offers. Whether you're seeking to witness time-honored papal ceremonies or take part in local traditions, this calendar will guide you through the heart of the Jubilee.

In this section, you'll find a detailed guide to all the major events of the Jubilee Year, including important dates, locations, and what you can expect from each one. Whether you're planning to be in Rome for a few days or the entire year, this calendar will ensure that you don't miss the key moments of spiritual significance that define the Holy Year of 2025.

Prepare to walk in the footsteps of millions of pilgrims before you as we guide you through the highlights of this sacred year and the events that make it unforgettable.

General Calendar

DECEMBER 2024

December 24: Opening of the Holy Door at the Basilica of St. Peter

JANUARY 2025

January 24-26: Jubilee of the World of Communication

FEBRUARY 2025

February 8-9: Jubilee of the Armed Forces, Police, and Security Forces

February 15-18: Jubilee of Artists

February 21-23: Jubilee of Deacons

MARCH 2025

March 8-9: Jubilee of the World of Volunteers

March 28: 24 Hours for the Lord

March 28-30: Jubilee of the Missionaries of Mercy

APRIL 2025

April 5-6: Jubilee of the Sick and the World of Healthcare

April 25-27: Jubilee of Adolescents

April 28-29: Jubilee of People with Disabilities

MAY 2025

May 1-4: Jubilee of Workers

May 4-5: Jubilee of Entrepreneurs

May 10-11: Jubilee of Musical Bands

May 12-14: Jubilee of the Eastern Churches

May 16-18: Jubilee of the Confraternities

May 30 - June 1: Jubilee of Families, Children, Grandparents, and Older Adults

JUNE 2025

June 7-8: Jubilee of Movements, Associations, and New Communities

June 9: Jubilee of the Holy See

June 14-15: Jubilee of Sports

June 20-22: Jubilee of Government Leaders

June 23-24: Jubilee of Seminarians

June 25: Jubilee of Bishops

June 25-27: Jubilee of Priests

JULY 2025

July 28 - August 3: Jubilee of Youth

SEPTEMBER 2025

September 15: Jubilee of Consolation

September 20: Jubilee of Justice Workers

September 26-28: Jubilee of Catechists

OCTOBER 2025

October 4-5: Jubilee of the Missionary World

October 4-5: Jubilee of Migrants

October 8-9: Jubilee of Consecrated Life

October 11-12: Jubilee of Marian Spirituality

October 31 - November 2: Jubilee of the World of Education

NOVEMBER 2025

November 16: Jubilee of the Poor

November 22-23: Jubilee of Choirs and Chorales

DECEMBER 2025

December 14: Jubilee of Prisoners

Important Notice to Readers: Disclaimer Regarding Jubilee Year 2025 Information

The information in this book regarding Jubilee Year 2025 events is accurate at the time of publication. However, please be aware that plans for the

Jubilee Year are subject to change and refinement as the event approaches and unfolds.

For the most current and accurate information about the Jubilee Year 2025, including up-to-date event schedules, registration details, and any changes to the program, we strongly encourage all readers to check the official Jubilee website regularly: www.iubilaeum2025.va

The official website will provide the latest announcements, adjustments to event dates or venues, and any new initiatives that may be added to the Jubilee calendar.

Although I've tried my best to give you complete and accurate information, the ever-changing nature of this significant event may result in updates or modifications to some details. Always refer to the official sources for the most reliable and current information as you plan your participation in the Jubilee Year 2025.

Your understanding and attention to this matter will ensure the best possible experience as you prepare for and take part in this momentous celebration of faith.

Attending Jubilee Events—General Information.

Accessibility Information: St. Peter's Square and most Jubilee churches are wheelchair accessible. For specific needs, contact: info2@iubilaeum2025.va

Additional Information

- Registration is required via the Jubilee Website.

- For any queries, contact: info2@iubilaeum2025.va

- Bishops and Priests wishing to celebrate the and Deacons wishing to participate in the Mass must book through the Office of Liturgical Celebrations of the Supreme Pontiff via this link: https://biglietti.liturgiepontificie.va/

The Jubilee of Modern Communication

From Pen to Pixel

Giubileo del Mondo della Comunicazione

Where: Basilica di San Pietro, Via delle Fondamenta, 00120, Città del Vaticano

When: January 24-26

The Jubilee of the World of Communication

One highlight of the 2025 Jubilee Year is the Jubilee of the World of Communication, scheduled for January 24-26, 2025. This event is particularly tailored for professionals in communication, including journalists, media operators, editors, board members, videographers, graphic designers, copywriters, PR professionals, social media managers, audio and video technicians, printers, and IT professionals.

Program Highlights:

Friday, January 24, 2025

17:30-19:00: Welcome and Penitential Liturgy

19:00: International Mass celebrating the feast of St. Francis de Sales at the Basilica of St. John Lateran

Saturday, January 25, 2025

8:00-9:30: Pilgrimage to the Holy Door of St. Peter's

9:00-10:00: Welcome Coffee Break in the Atrium of Paul VI Hall

10:00: Cultural meeting "In dialogue with Maria Ressa and Colum McCann," moderated by Mario Calabresi in Paul VI Hall, featuring a performance by Maestro Uto Ughi

12:30: Meeting with the Holy Father in Paul VI Hall

15:00-16:30: Dialogue with the city: cultural and spiritual meetings on various themes related to communication and hope, held in different locations across Rome

Sunday, January 26, 2025

10:00: "Sunday of the Word of God" Mass presided over by the Holy Father in St. Peter's Basilica, including the institution of new lectors

Registration Deadline: November 24, 2024.

Guardians of Peace

Rome's Jubilee for the Armed Forces, Police and Security Services

Giubileo delle Forze Armate, di Polizia e di Sicurezza

Where: Various locations in Rome, including Piazza del Popolo and St. Peter's Square

When: February 8-9, 2025

The Jubilee for Armed Forces, Police, and Security Services

This unique gathering brings together members of the military, police forces, urban guards, security operators, veterans, various military associations, military academies, and military chaplaincies and ordinariates, along with their families.

Timeline of Events

The Jubilee for Armed Forces, Police, and Security Services unfolds over two days:

Saturday: All-day pilgrimage to the Holy Door and evening welcome concert

Sunday: Mass presided over by the Pope in St. Peter's Square

Register by December 8, 2024, to secure your place.

Divine Inspirations

Celebrating Art and Soul at the Jubilee of Artists

Giubileo degli Artisti

Where: Basilica di San Pietro in Vaticano and various locations in Rome

When: February 15-18, 2025

The Jubilee of Artists

Within the framework of the Jubilee Year 2025, Rome hosts a special gathering celebrating the unique relationship between the Church and the world of art. This event brings together artists from various disciplines, recognizing their role as visionaries and prophets who can "dream up new versions of the world" and "introduce novelty into history."

History and Significance

Art and the Church have a timeless connection, inspiring masterpieces of faith. This Jubilee event builds on that rich history while looking to the future. It reflects Pope Francis' vision of artists as "sentinels" who can discern deeper realities and help humanity experience the divine through beauty.

On June 23, 2023, commemorating the 50th anniversary of the Vatican Museums' Collection of Modern and Contemporary Art, Pope Francis addressed artists in the Sistine Chapel, emphasizing their prophetic role and ability to inspire a desire for God through true beauty.

Key Events

Art Exhibitions: Showcasing works that explore themes of faith, hope, and human experience

Performances: Music, dance, and theatrical presentations in sacred spaces

Workshops: Exploring the intersection of art and spirituality

Papal Address: Anticipated words from Pope Francis on the role of art in faith and society

Interfaith Dialogue: Discussions on art's role in different religious traditions

Local Customs and Traditions:

- Blessing of artists' tools: A tradition where artists' instruments and materials are blessed. And creation of collaborative works.

- Art in sacred spaces: Temporary installations in Rome's churches and religious sites

Servants of the World

Honoring Faith and Charity in the Jubilee of Deacons

Giubileo dei Diaconi

Where: St. Peter's Square and various jubilee churches in Rome

When: February 21-23, 2025

The Jubilee of Deacons

In conjunction with the Jubilee Year 2025, Rome welcomes permanent deacons and their families for a special celebration of their vital role in the Church. This event recognizes the unique ministry of deacons who serve as a bridge between the clergy and the laity.

History and Significance

The diaconate is one of the oldest ministries in the Church, dating back to apostolic times. This Jubilee event highlights the renewed emphasis on the permanent diaconate since the Second Vatican Council, celebrating their service in liturgy, word, and charity.

Timeline of Events

The Jubilee of Deacons unfolds over three days:

Friday, February 21, 2025

15:30: Welcome and communal recitation of Midday Prayer in jubilee churches, divided by language

16:00-18:00: Catechesis and sharing of experiences

Saturday, February 22, 2025

8:00-17:00: Pilgrimage to the Holy Door with the opportunity to receive the Sacrament of Reconciliation in jubilee churches

18:00: Vocational vigil in jubilee churches, divided by language

Sunday, February 23, 2025

10:00: Mass presided over by the Holy Father in St. Peter's Square, including diaconal ordinations

Register by December 21, 2024.

Pay the €20 solidarity fee to support deacons needing assistance to attend.

Acts of Mercy

Celebrating Volunteers, Social Workers and NonProfit Organizations

Giubileo del Mondo del Volontariato

Where: Basilica di San Pietro in Vaticano

When: March 8–9, 2025

Jubilee of the World of Volunteering

This jubilee event extends a special invitation to all volunteers from every association, members of non-profit organizations, NGO operators, and social workers.

Saturday, March 8

8:00 AM - 6:00 PM: Pilgrimage to the Holy Door

3:00 PM - 6:00 PM: Dialogue with the city: Cultural, artistic, and spiritual activities

Sunday, March 9

10:30 AM: Holy Mass presided over by the Holy Father (St. Peter's Square)

Registration Deadline: January 5, 2025.

Messengers of Mercy

A Jubilee Compassion and Renewal

Giubileo dei Missionari della Misericordia

Where: Basilica di San Pietro in Vaticano

When: March 28–30, 2025

Jubilee of the Missionaries of Mercy

The Missionaries of Mercy's Jubilee is a profound celebration of individuals appointed to be living signs of God's mercy. This event, situated at the center of Vatican City, underscores the importance of mercy and forgiveness in the Christian faith and our global society.

By gathering Missionaries of Mercy from every corner of the globe, the Church acknowledges its crucial role in bringing God's compassion to all corners of the Earth. This jubilee offers participants a unique opportunity to reflect on their mission, renew their commitment to mercy, and draw inspiration from their shared experiences and faith.

Friday, March 28

9:00 AM: Opening Prayer

9:30 AM - 10:00 AM: Formation Moment - First Session (Aula Paolo VI)

10:30 AM: Coffee Break

11:00 AM - 11:30 AM: Formation Moment - Second Session (Aula Paolo VI)

4:00 PM - 5:00 PM: Celebration of "24 Hours for the Lord"

In jubilee churches, divided by language,

Saturday, March 29

9:00 AM - 11:00 AM: Pilgrimage to the Holy Door of St. Peter's

Noon: Meeting with the Holy Father (Aula Paolo VI)

Sunday, March 30

10:00 AM: Holy Mass

6:00 PM: Symphonic Concert "Missa Papae Francisci" (Church of Sant'Ignazio)

Registration Deadline: January 26, 2025

Healing Hearts and Hands

The Jubilee of the Sick and the World of Healthcare

Giubileo degli Ammalati e del Mondo della Sanità

Where: Basilica di San Pietro in Vaticano

When: April 5-6, 2025

The Jubilee of the Sick and the World of Healthcare

As a component of the Jubilee Year 2025, Rome hosts a special gathering, celebrating the profound connection between faith, healing, and compassionate care. This event brings together the sick, their families, and healthcare professionals, recognizing the sacred nature of healing and the importance of holistic care for the body, mind, and spirit.

Religious orders were founded to care for the sick and vulnerable, showcasing the Church's extensive involvement in healthcare. This Jubilee event builds on that rich tradition while addressing contemporary challenges in healthcare. It reflects Pope Francis' emphasis on the "culture of care" and the importance of treating each patient with dignity and compassion.

Saturday, April 5

8:00 AM - 5:00 PM: Pilgrimage to the Holy Door • Opportunity to receive the Sacrament of Reconciliation in the Jubilee churches

4:00 PM - 6:30 PM: Dialogue with the city: Cultural, artistic, and spiritual activities • Taking place in various squares throughout Rome

Sunday, April 6. 10:30 AM: Holy Mass presided over by the Holy Father (St. Peter's Square)

Local Customs and Traditions

- Blessing of the Sick: A tradition where the ill receive a special blessing

- Anointing of the Sick: Sacrament may be offered to those who are seriously ill

- Prayer vigils: Communities may organize prayer sessions for healing and strength

Register by February 9, 2025.

St. Peter's Square and Basilica are wheelchair accessible

Special arrangements may be made for those with serious illnesses or disabilities

Contact organizers for specific needs: info2@iubilaeum2025.va

Youthful Hearts, Jubilant Spirits

Celebrating the Jubilee of Teenagers

Giubileo degli Adolescenti

Where: Basilica di San Pietro in Vaticano and various locations in Rome

When: April 25-27, 2025

The Jubilee of Teenagers

This event is particularly designed for boys and girls aged 12 to 17, offering them a unique opportunity to experience the universal Church and deepen their faith in the heart of Rome.

Friday, April 25: 9:00 AM - 6:00 PM: Pilgrimage to the Holy Door • Opportunity to receive the Sacrament of Reconciliation in the Jubilee churches

6:00 PM - 7:30 PM: Prayer of the Via Lucis (stations of the Resurrection and Pentecost)

Saturday, April 26: 8:00 AM - 6:00 PM: Pilgrimage to the Holy Door • Opportunity to receive the Sacrament of Reconciliation in the Jubilee churches

11:00 AM - 3:00 PM: Moments of animation (concerts, prayers, themed gatherings, testimonies) in various Rome city squares

5:30 PM - 7:00 PM: Moment of musical celebration

Sunday, April 27

10:30 AM: Holy Mass presided over by the Holy Father (St. Peter's Square) • Some teenagers will receive the sacrament of Confirmation from the Holy Father

Register by January 31, 2025

Full payment due by March 15, 2025

Empowered Grace

The Jubilee for People with Disabilities

Giubileo delle Persone con Disabilita

Where: St. Peter's Square and various locations in Rome

When: April 28-29, 2025

Average Temperatures: High 20°C (68°F), Low 10°C (50°F)

The Jubilee of People with Disabilities

Monday, April 28, 2025

8:00-17:00: Pilgrimage to the Holy Door • with the opportunity to receive the Sacrament of Reconciliation in jubilee churches

17:00: Celebration of Holy Mass (St. Peter's Square)

Tuesday, April 29, 2025: 11:00: Meeting with the Holy Father (St. Peter's Square)

13:00: Welcome lunch for all participants (Gardens of Castel Sant'Angelo)

15:00-19:00: Festive gathering (Gardens of Castel Sant'Angelo)

Register by February 23, 2025

Divine Labor

Celebrating the Dignity of Work in the Jubilee Year

Giubileo dei Lavoratori

Where: Basilica di San Pietro in Vaticano and various locations in Rome

When: May 1-4, 2025

The Jubilee of Workers

Considering the Jubilee Year 2025, Rome hosts a special gathering, celebrating workers of all categories, along with their families, trade associations, and unions. The event honors the significance of work in our lives and society.

Timeline of Events

The Jubilee of Workers unfolds over four days, featuring:

May 1 (Thursday):

8:00 AM - 12:00 PM: Pilgrimage to the Holy Door

Opportunity for Reconciliation Sacrament in jubilee churches

3:00 PM - 12:00 AM: May Day Concert (Piazza S. Giovanni in Laterano)

Organized by the three main Italian trade union confederations (CGIL, CISL, and UIL)

May 2 (Friday)

8:00 AM - 6:00 PM: Pilgrimage to the Holy Door

Opportunity for Reconciliation Sacrament in jubilee churches

10:00 AM - 6:00 PM: Welcome events with Rome's working world

May 3 (Saturday)

8:00 AM - 6:00 PM: Pilgrimage to the Holy Door

Opportunity for Reconciliation Sacrament in jubilee churches

11:00 AM - 3:00 PM: Dialogue with the city: cultural, artistic, and spiritual activities

In various squares of Rome

May 4 (Sunday)

10:30 AM: Holy Mass presided over by the Holy Father (St. Peter's Square)

Registration deadline: March 2, 2025

Visionary Leadership

Entrepreneurs' Path to Purpose in the Jubilee Year

Giubileo degli Imprenditori

Where: Basilica di San Pietro in Vaticano and Aula Paolo VI

When: May 4-5, 2025

The Jubilee of Entrepreneurs

As a component of the Jubilee Year 2025, Rome hosts a special gathering for entrepreneurs, recognizing their role in shaping economies and societies.

May 4 (Sunday)

10:30 AM: Holy Mass presided over by the Holy Father (St. Peter's Square)

May 5 (Monday)

9:30 AM - 11:00 AM: Pilgrimage to the Holy Door of St. Peter's

10:30 AM - 11:30 AM: Welcome Moment (Atrium of Paul VI Audience Hall)

Noon: Catechesis by the Holy Father with the entrepreneurial world (Paul VI Audience Hall)

Registration deadline: March 2, 2025

Melodies of Faith

Bands Uniting Rome in Jubilee Celebration

Giubileo delle Bande Musicali

Where: Piazza del Popolo and various locations in Rome

When: May 10-11, 2025

The Jubilee of Music Bands

The Giubileo delle Bande Musicali is a jubilant celebration of the universal language of music, set against the backdrop of the Eternal City during the Jubilee Year 2025. This unique event gathers music bands from across the globe to showcase their talents and express their faith through melodies that transcend cultural and geographical boundaries.

Participants include military bands, institutional ensembles, amateur groups, folkloric and village bands, as well as those from schools, colleges, and sports organizations. The event invites not only the musicians but also their families, creating an atmosphere of unity and shared joy.

Over the two days, the city of Rome transforms into a vibrant stage where music resounds from its historic squares and streets, fostering a deep sense of community and spiritual reflection through the art of sound.

May 10 (Saturday)

8:00 AM - 6:00 PM: Pilgrimage to the Holy Door

4:00 PM - 7:30 PM: Band performances in various squares of Rome

May 11 (Sunday)

10:30 AM: Holy Mass presided over by the Holy Father (St. Peter's Square)

Registration deadline: March 9, 2025.

Unity in Diversity

Celebrating the Eastern Churches in the Jubilee Year

Giubileo delle Chiese Orientali

Where: St. Peter's Basilica, Vatican City

When: May 12-14, 2025

The Jubilee of Eastern Churches

As part of the Jubilee Year 2025, Rome extends a special welcome to members of the Eastern Catholic Churches. This event celebrates the rich diversity within the Catholic Church, highlighting the unique liturgical traditions, spirituality, and cultural heritage of the Eastern Churches in communion with Rome.

Significance

This Jubilee event emphasizes the universality of the Catholic Church, showcasing the beauty of different rites and traditions while affirming the unity of faith. It serves as a reminder of the Church's commitment to preserving and honoring diverse expressions of the same Catholic faith.

This event will honor the rich spiritual traditions of the Eastern Catholic Churches, emphasizing their unique liturgical practices and cultural heritage within the universal Church.

While specific details of the program are yet to be announced, participants can anticipate a series of liturgical celebrations, cultural exchanges, and opportunities for deepening ecumenical dialogue.

For the most current information and updates on the Jubilee of the Eastern Churches, please refer to the official Jubilee 2025 website.

Brotherhood in Faith

Celebrating Catholic Confraternities

Giubileo delle Confraternite

Where: Basilica di San Pietro in Vaticano and various locations in Rome

When: May 16-18

Jubilee of the Brotherhoods

Understanding Catholic Confraternities

Catholic confraternities are lay organizations that trace their roots to medieval Europe. These brotherhoods and sisterhoods play a vital role in Catholic life by combining religious devotion with community service. Members participate in religious processions, care for local shrines and chapels, and engage in charitable work. Within Catholic communities, confraternities help preserve local religious traditions while fostering fellowship among believers.

The Jubilee Celebration

The Jubilee gathering in Rome brings confraternity members together from around the world. This special event allows these groups to showcase their unique traditions, exchange experiences with fellow members, and deepen their spiritual commitments through shared celebration.

Timeline of Events

The Jubilee of Confraternities unfolds over three days

May 16 (Friday)

8:00 AM - 5:00 PM: Pilgrimage to the Holy Door

Opportunity for Reconciliation Sacrament in jubilee churches

5:00 PM - 6:30 PM: Welcome Event by the Confraternities of Rome

May 17 (Saturday)

8:00 AM - 5:00 PM: Pilgrimage to the Holy Door

Opportunity for Reconciliation Sacrament in jubilee churches

From 5:00 PM: Grand Procession through the streets of Rome

May 18 (Sunday)

10:30 AM: Holy Mass presided over by the Holy Father (St. Peter's Square)

Registration deadline: March 16

United in Faith

A celebration of Family, Children, & Grandparents

Giubileo delle Famiglie, dei Bambini, dei Nonni e degli Anziani

Where: Basilica di San Pietro in Vaticano and various locations in Rome

When: May 30 - June 1, 2025

The Jubilee of Families, Children, Grandparents, and the Elderly

This special Jubilee event celebrates the family in all its generations, recognizing the unique roles and contributions of each family member in the fabric of faith and society.

May 30 (Friday): 8:00 AM - 6:00 PM: Pilgrimage to the Holy Door

Opportunity for Reconciliation Sacrament in jubilee churches

4:00 PM - 7:30 PM: "Living joy in the family, following the example of the Martin family. ,"

Concert, shows, and games for children, veneration of the relics of St. Therese of Lisieux and the Martin couple (Church of SS. Trinità dei Monti)

6:00 PM: "Not 'how', but 'what'. The surprise of gratuitousness."

Panel exhibition (Cloister of S. Salvatore in Lauro)

9:00 PM: Prayer Vigil (Church of SS. Trinità dei Monti)

May 31 (Saturday): 8:00 AM - 6:00 PM: Pilgrimage to the Holy Door

10:00 AM - 12:00 PM: "The value of old age"

Catechesis on the theme of aging (Basilica of S. Maria in Trastevere)

10:00 AM - 12:00 PM: Animation moments in various squares of Rome

10:00 AM - 1:00 PM: "The Family Global Compact and the international network of family associations,"

6:30 PM - 8:00 PM: "Family Festival" and Prayer Vigil (Piazza S. Giovanni in Laterano)

June 1 (Sunday): 10:30 AM: Holy Mass presided over by the Holy Father (St. Peter's Square)

Registration deadline: March 30, 2025

Ecclesial Movement

Celebration of Associations and Communities

Giubileo dei Movimenti, delle Associazioni e delle nuove Comunità

Where: Basilica di San Pietro in Vaticano

When: June 7-8, 2025

The Jubilee of Movements, Associations, and New Communities

This special Jubilee event invites all members of ecclesial movements, associations, new communities, and prayer groups to come together in Rome. It celebrates the diverse expressions of faith within the Catholic Church and the vital role these groups play in the life and mission of the Church.

Understanding Ecclesial Movements and New Communities

Ecclesial movements and new communities are groups of Catholics, often lay-led, that have emerged, especially since the Second Vatican Council.

They offer fresh approaches to living out the Catholic faith, often with specific charisms or focuses. These groups range from contemplative prayer communities to active social justice organizations, representing the Church's diversity and vitality.

Timeline of Events

The Jubilee unfolds over two days, coinciding with the Pentecost celebration:

June 7 (Saturday): 8:00 AM - 6:00 PM: Pilgrimage to the Holy Door

Opportunity for Reconciliation Sacrament in jubilee churches

6:00 PM - 8:00 PM: Pre-Vigil (St. Peter's Square)

8:00 PM - 9:00 PM: Pentecost Vigil presided over by the Holy Father (St. Peter's Square)

June 8 (Sunday - Pentecost): 9:30 AM: Holy Mass presided over by the Holy Father (St. Peter's Square)

Significance of Pentecost

The timing of this Jubilee event with Pentecost is particularly meaningful. Pentecost commemorates the descent of the Holy Spirit upon the Apostles and other followers of Jesus, often considered the birthday of the Church. It's a fitting time for diverse groups within the Church to come together, reflecting the unity in diversity that characterizes both Pentecost and the modern Church.

Registration deadline: April 6, 2025

Servants of the Universal Church

Celebrating the Vatican and Vatican Institutions

Giubileo della Santa Sede

Where: Basilica di San Pietro in Vaticano

When: April 5-6, 2025

The Jubilee of the Holy See

This special Jubilee event is dedicated to the Holy See, the universal government of the Catholic Church. It brings together those who serve the Church in various capacities within the Vatican and related institutions.

April 5 (Saturday): 8:00 AM - 6:00 PM: Pilgrimage to the Holy Door

Opportunity for Reconciliation Sacrament in jubilee churches

Additional events may be scheduled (details to be announced)

April 6 (Sunday): 10:30 AM: Holy Mass presided over by the Holy Father (St. Peter's Square)

Registration deadline: February 2, 2025

Faith in Motion

Celebrating Unity, Excellence, and the Jubilee of the World of Sports

Giubileo dello Sport

Where: Basilica di San Pietro in Vaticano and Piazza del Popolo

When: June 14-15, 2025

The Jubilee of Sport

This special Jubilee event celebrates the world of sport and its connection to faith and values. It invites all those involved in sports - athletes, amateurs, coaches, sports directors, sports associations, and their families - to come together in Rome for a unique celebration of physical prowess and spiritual reflection.

Participants

This Jubilee event particularly welcomes:

- Professional and amateur athletes

- Coaches and trainers. Sports directors and administrators.

- Members of sports associations

- Families of those involved in sports

Timeline of Events

The Jubilee unfolds over two days:

June 14 (Saturday)

9:00 AM: Welcome Moment

10:00 AM - 5:00 PM: Sports Village (Piazza del Popolo)

"Sport generates hope": Meeting with big names in sports

Following the Sports Village: "Pilgrimage of Hope" towards the Holy Door of St. Peter's Basilica

June 15 (Sunday)

9:30 AM: Holy Mass presided over by the Holy Father (St. Peter's Square)

Sports Village: A day-long celebration of sport featuring:

- Encounters with famous athletes

- Exhibitions by sports associations

- Discussions on the theme "Sport generates hope."

Registration Deadline: April 20, 2025

Leadership and Faith

Honoring Leaders in the Jubilee of Governors

Giubileo dei Governanti

Where: Basilica di San Pietro in Vaticano

When: June 19-22, 2025

The Jubilee of Governors

This special Jubilee event is dedicated to those in positions of governmental leadership.

Participants include Heads of State and Government, Ministers and high-ranking government officials, Diplomats, and Local government leaders.

The Jubilee of Governors is scheduled for June 19–22, 2025, in Rome, with events primarily at the Basilica of St. Peter in the Vatican.

Provisional Program:

- Thursday, June 19, 2025

  - Interparliamentary Conference on Interfaith Dialogue.

- Friday, June 20, 2025

  - Interparliamentary Conference on Interfaith Dialogue.

- Saturday, June 21, 2025

  - Interparliamentary Conference on Interfaith Dialogue.

  - Pilgrimage to the Holy Door with opportunities for the Sacrament of Reconciliation in the Jubilee churches.

- Sunday, June 22, 2025

  - Holy Mass presided over by the Holy Father in St. Peter's Basilica at 10:00 AM.

Future Shephards

A Celebration of Faith, Dedication, and the Jubilee of Seminarians

Giubileo dei Seminaristi

Where: Basilica di San Pietro in Vaticano and other locations in Rome

When: June 23-24, 2025 (with an additional event on June 26)

The Jubilee of Seminarians

This special Jubilee event is dedicated to seminarians coming from various parts of the world, offering them a unique opportunity to gather in Rome, deepen their faith, and reflect on their vocational journey.

The Jubilee unfolds over two principal days, with an additional event two days later:

June 23 (Monday): From 5:00 PM: Welcome meeting with all seminarians and communal recitation of First Vespers of St. John (Basilica of St. John Lateran)

June 24 (Tuesday):

9:00 AM: Catechesis with the Holy Father (St. Peter's Square)

10:00 AM - 12:30 PM: Pilgrimage to the Holy Door of St. Peter's

5:30 PM - 7:30 PM: Moments of sharing and celebration (Gardens of Castel Sant'Angelo)

June 26 (Thursday):

7:00 PM - 9:00 PM: Vocational vigil (St. Peter's Square)

Key Events

- First Vespers of St. John: A communal prayer experience to begin the Jubilee

- Catechesis with the Pope: An opportunity for direct teaching from the Holy Father

- Pilgrimage to the Holy Door: A spiritual journey symbolizing renewal and commitment

- Celebrations in multiple languages: Recognizing the universal nature of the Church

- Sharing and festive moments: Building community among seminarians

- Vocational vigil: A prayerful reflection on the call to priesthood

Registration deadline: April 20, 2025

Solidarity fee: €20

Shepherds of the Catholic Faith

The Bishop's Jubilee

Giubileo dei Vescovi

Where: Basilica di San Giovanni in Laterano and Piazza San Pietro

When: June 25-26, 2025

The Jubilee of Bishops

This special Jubilee event is dedicated to the bishops of the Catholic Church, offering them a unique opportunity to gather in Rome, renew their faith, and reflect on their role as shepherds of the Church.

June 25 (Wednesday): 9:30 AM - 11:00 AM: Pilgrimage to the Holy Door of St. John Lateran

Communal profession of the professio fidei (Profession of Faith)

Noon: Meditation by the Holy Father (Basilica of St. John Lateran)

June 26 (Thursday): 7:00 PM - 9:00 PM: Vocational vigil (St. Peter's Square)

The Basilica of St. John Lateran

Registration deadline: April 20, 2025

Servants of the Faithful

Celebrating Leadership and Unity in the Jubilee of Bishops

Giubileo dei Sacerdoti

Where: Basilica di San Pietro in Vaticano and other locations in Rome

When: June 25-27, 2025

The Jubilee of Priests

This special Jubilee event is dedicated to priests from around the world, offering them a unique opportunity to gather in Rome, renew their vocation, and celebrate their ministry in the Church.

June 25 (Wednesday): 5:30 PM - 6:30 PM: Welcome moment by the presbytery of Rome (Piazza S. Giovanni in Laterano)

June 26 (Thursday): 8:00 AM - 6:00 PM: Pilgrimage to the Holy Door

7:00 PM - 9:00 PM: Vocational vigil (St. Peter's Square)

June 27 (Friday): 9:30 AM: Holy Mass presided over by the Holy Father (St. Peter's Square)

Registration deadline: April 20, 2025

Solidarity fee: €50

Faith in the Digital Age

Jubilee of Missionaries and Influencers

Giubileo dei missionari digitali e degli influencer cattolici

Where: To be announced (likely in Rome)

When: July 28-29, 2025

The Jubilee of Digital Missionaries and Catholic Influencers

This innovative Jubilee event recognizes the growing importance of digital media in spreading the Gospel and nurturing faith communities. It brings together those who use digital platforms to share the Catholic faith and values.

Significance

This Jubilee event highlights the Catholic Church's recognition of the digital world as a crucial mission field in the 21st century. It acknowledges that:

- Digital platforms offer new ways to reach people with the Gospel message

- Online communities can provide support and nurture faith

- Digital tools can enhance religious education and spiritual growth

- Social media influencers can be modern-day evangelists

This event aligns with recent papal messages for World Communications Day, which have increasingly focused on the role of digital media in faith and community building. It reflects the Church's effort to engage with modern means of communication while maintaining the integrity of its message.

Check the official Jubilee website for details on the program once it is available.

Comfort and Compassion

A Celebration of Healing and Faith in the Jubilee of Consolation

Giubileo della Consolazione

Where: Basilica di San Pietro in Vaticano (St. Peter's Basilica, Vatican)

When: September 15, 2025

Event Type: Grande Evento (Major Event)

Jubilee of Consolation

The Giubileo della Consolazione is a special jubilee event dedicated to those experiencing times of sorrow and affliction. This event particularly invites individuals, along with their families and friends, who are going through periods of pain because of illness, bereavement, violence, or abuse.

Monday, September 15, 2025

8:00-18:00: Pilgrimage to the Holy Door

17:00: "Ridare speranza, asciugando le lacrime" (Restoring hope, wiping away tears)

Prayer vigil with the Holy Father in St. Peter's Basilica

Register by July 13, 2025

Justice and Grace

Upholding Faith and Fairness in the Jubilee of Justice

Giubileo degli Operatori di Giustizia

Where: Basilica di San Pietro in Vaticano (St. Peter's Basilica, Vatican) and Aula Paolo VI (Paul VI Audience Hall)

When: September 20, 2025

Event Type: Grande Evento (Major Event)

Jubilee of Justice

The Giubileo degli Operatori di Giustizia is a special jubilee event dedicated to those involved in the world of secular, canonical, and ecclesiastical justice. This event particularly invites individuals, along with their families, who work in various capacities within the justice system, including judges, prosecutors, magistrates, lawyers, and legal professionals.

Saturday, September 20, 2025

9:00-11:30: Pilgrimage to the Holy Door. Opportunity to receive the Sacrament of Reconciliation in jubilee churches

Noon: Catechesis with the Holy Father (Paul VI Audience Hall)

Register by July 20, 2025

Nuturing the Faith

The Volunteers and Teachers Jubilee

Giubileo dei Catechisti

Where: Basilica di San Pietro in Vaticano (St. Peter's Basilica, Vatican), Piazza San Giovanni, and various jubilee churches

When: September 26-28, 2025

Jubilee of Catechists

Who is a Catechist?

A catechist is a person who teaches and shares the Catholic faith, often volunteering their time to instruct others in religious education programs, sacramental preparation, and other faith-based initiatives. They play a vital role in fostering spiritual growth and understanding within their communities, guiding individuals of all ages in their journey of faith.

This event particularly invites these individuals, along with their families, to participate in a weekend of spiritual renewal.

Friday, September 26, 2025. 8:00-18:00: Pilgrimage to the Holy Door

18:30-19:30: Welcome and reception by the Diocese of Rome (Piazza San Giovanni)

Saturday, September 27, 2025. 8:00-18:00: Pilgrimage to the Holy Door

16:30-18:30: Catechesis sessions in jubilee churches, divided by language

Sunday, September 28, 2025. 10:30: Holy Mass presided over by the Holy Father (St. Peter's Square)

Register by July 20, 2025

Spreading the Gospel

Celebrating Service and Unity in the Jubilee of the Missionary World

Giubileo del Mondo Missionario

Where: Basilica di San Pietro in Vaticano (St. Peter's Basilica, Vatican) and various locations in Rome

When: October 4-5, 2025

Event Type: Grande Evento (Major Event)

Jubilee of the Missionary World

This event invites missionaries, those supporting mission work, and all faithful interested in the Church's global evangelization efforts.

The Jubilee of the Missionary World is scheduled for October 4–5, 2025, in Rome, with events at St. Peter's Square, St. Peter's Basilica, Basilica of St. Paul Outside the Walls, and the Urbaniana University.

Program Highlights:

- Saturday, October 4, 2025:

  - 10:00 AM: Meeting with the Holy Father in St. Peter's Square.

  - 12:00 PM: Pilgrimage to the Holy Door of St. Peter's Basilica.

  - 6:00 PM: Concert by the Republic Bank Exodus Steel Orchestra from Trinidad and Tobago.

- Sunday, October 5, 2025:

  - 10:30 AM: Holy Mass presided over by Cardinal Luis Antonio Tagle, Pro-Prefect of the Dicastery for Evangelization, at the Basilica of St. Paul Outside the Walls.

  - 4:00 PM: International Missionary Meeting in the Aula Magna of the Urbaniana University

Registration Details:

- **Deadline:** August 3, 2025

Bridging Borders

Celebrating Unity and Resilience in the Jubilee of Migrants

Giubileo dei Migranti

Where:

- Basilica di San Pietro in Vaticano (St. Peter's Basilica, Vatican)

- Basilica di San Paolo Fuori le mura (Basilica of Saint Paul Outside the Walls)

- Giardini di Castel Sant'Angelo (Castel Sant'Angelo Gardens)

When: October 4-5, 2025

Event Type: Grande Evento (Major Event)

Jubilee of Migrants

Saturday, October 4, 2025. 8:00-18:00: Pilgrimage to the Holy Door

10:00: Meeting with the Holy Father (St. Peter's Square)

Sunday, October 5, 2025. 15:00-18:00: Festive gathering (Castel Sant'Angelo Gardens)

Register by August 3, 2025

Vows of Faith

Celebrating Devotion in the Jubilee of Consecrated Life

Giubileo della Vita Consacrata

Where:

- Basilica di San Pietro in Vaticano (St. Peter's Basilica, Vatican)

- Piazza di San Giovanni in Laterano (St. John Lateran Square)

When: October 8-9, 2025

Event Type: Grande Evento (Major Event)

Jubilee of Consecrated Life

The Giubileo della Vita Consacrata is a special jubilee event dedicated to those in consecrated life.

Wednesday, October 8, 2025

8:00-18:00: Pilgrimage to the Holy Door

15:00-17:00: Dialogue with the city. 18:30-20:00: Prayer Vigil (St. John Lateran Square)

Thursday, October 9. 10:30: Holy Mass presided over by the Holy Father (St. Peter's Square)

Register by August 3, 2025

Mary's Light

A Celebration of Devotion in the Jubilee of Marian Spirituality

Giubileo della Spiritualità Mariana

Where:

- Basilica di San Pietro in Vaticano (St. Peter's Basilica, Vatican)

- Basilica di Santa Maria Maggiore (Basilica of Saint Mary Major)

When: October 11-12, 2025

Event Type: Grande Evento (Major Event)

Jubilee of Marian Spirituality

This event particularly invites all rectors and staff of Marian shrines, members of Marian movements, confraternities, and various Marian prayer groups to participate in a two-day celebration of devotion to the Blessed Virgin Mary.

Saturday, October 11, 2025. 8:00-17:00: Pilgrimage to the Holy Door

17:00-19:00: Prayer Vigil (Basilica of Saint Mary Major)

Sunday, October 12, 2025. 10:30: Holy Mass presided over by the Holy Father (St. Peter's Square)

Register by August 10, 2025

Illuminating Minds and Hearts

Jubilee of the World of Education

Giubileo del Mondo Educativo

Where: Basilica di San Pietro in Vaticano (St. Peter's Basilica, Vatican)

When: October 31 - November 2, 2025

Event Type: Grande Evento (Major Event)

Jubilee of the Educational World

The Giubileo del Mondo Educativo is a special jubilee event dedicated to the world of education. This event will bring together educators, students, and those involved in education for reflection, celebration, and renewal.

Events primarily at St. Peter's Basilica and the Basilica of Santa Maria degli Angeli.
Friday, October 31

Educational Village: Opening at the Basilica of Santa Maria degli Angeli, featuring interactive exhibits and discussions on contemporary educational challenges and innovations.

Saturday, November 1

Educational Village: Continued activities at the Basilica of Santa Maria degli Angeli.

Sunday, November 2

10:30 AM: Holy Mass presided over by the Holy Father in St. Peter's Square, bringing together educators, students, and stakeholders in the educational sector for a collective celebration of faith and learning.

Registration deadline not listed at time of printing.

Embracing Grace

Blessed are the Poor: A Jubilee of Compassion and Dignity

Giubileo dei Poveri

Where: Basilica di San Pietro in Vaticano (St. Peter's Basilica, Vatican)

When: November 16, 2025

Event Type: Grande Evento (Major Event)

Jubilee of the Poor

The Giubileo dei Poveri is a special jubilee event dedicated to people with low incomes and those who serve them. This event is likely to focus on the Church's commitment to social justice, charity, and the preferential option for the poor. Stay tuned for more details on this powerful jubilee, which aims to show solidarity with the marginalized and reflect on the Christian call to serve the needy.

Timeline of events not posted at time of printing.

Choruses of Joy

A Harmony of Faith in the Jubilee of Choirs

Giubileo dei Cori e delle Corali

Where:

- Basilica di San Pietro in Vaticano (St. Peter's Basilica, Vatican)

- Various churches and parishes in Rome

When: November 22-23, 2025

Event Type: Grande Evento (Major Event)

Jubilee of Choirs and Chorales

The Giubileo dei Cori e delle Corali is a special jubilee event dedicated to choirs and hymns. This event brings together choral groups to celebrate the rich tradition of sacred music in the Church and to offer their talents in praise and worship.

Saturday, November 22, 2025: 8:00-18:00: Pilgrimage to the Holy Door

17:00-19:30: Animation of evening Masses (with last concerts) in various churches and parishes of Rome

Sunday, November 23, 2025: 10:30: Holy Mass presided over by the Holy Father (St. Peter's Square)

Register by September 21, 2025

Mercy and Forgiveness

A Celebration of Redemption in the Jubilee of Prisoners

Giubileo dei Detenuti

Where: Basilica di San Pietro in Vaticano (St. Peter's Basilica, Vatican)

When: December 14, 2025

Event Type: Grande Evento (Major Event)

Jubilee of Prisoners

The Giubileo dei Detenuti is a special jubilee event dedicated to prisoners, and those involved in prison ministry. This unique event offers an opportunity for spiritual renewal and reflection on themes of justice, mercy, and rehabilitation within the context of faith.

Program Details:

- 9:00 AM: Pilgrimage to the Holy Door of St. Peter's Basilica, with opportunities for the Sacrament of Reconciliation.

- 10:00 AM: Holy Mass presided over by the Holy Father in St. Peter's Basilica.

Registration Information:

- Deadline: October 12, 2025.

CHAPTER TWENTY-THREE

Taste of Rome

Traditional Roman Fare and Dining Recommendations by Area

R ome isn't just a feast for the eyes, with its ancient monuments and stunning architecture—it's also a feast for the palate. The Eternal City boasts a rich culinary tradition that combines simple, fresh ingredients with bold flavors, creating dishes that have been cherished for centuries. From hearty pastas to crispy fried snacks, every meal in Rome tells a story of history, culture, and passion. Whether you're wandering the cobblestone streets or sitting at a traditional trattoria, these iconic Roman dishes offer a taste of the city's soul, inviting you to indulge in its timeless flavors.

Cacio e Pepe. A simple yet delicious pasta dish made with just three ingredients: pecorino romano cheese, freshly cracked black pepper, and pasta (usually tonnarelli or spaghetti). The heat from the pasta melts the cheese, creating a creamy, peppery sauce that clings to the noodles.

Why try it?: It's a perfect example of Roman cuisine's ability to create extraordinary flavor from humble ingredients.

Carbonara. Another iconic Roman pasta, carbonara is made with guanciale (cured pork cheek), pecorino romano, eggs, and black pepper. The eggs create a rich, creamy sauce (without any cream) that coats the pasta, usually spaghetti or rigatoni.

Why try it?: A must-try for any pasta lover, carbonara is Roman comfort food at its finest, with the guanciale adding a savory, crispy contrast to the creamy sauce.

Amatriciana. A classic pasta sauce made with guanciale, tomatoes, and pecorino romano cheese. Bucatini, a thick, hollow pasta, is traditionally used to absorb the robust flavors of the sauce.

Why try it?: Amatriciana is a rich and tangy dish that balances the salty pork with the sweetness of tomatoes, showcasing the depth of Roman pasta traditions.

Saltimbocca alla Romana. Thin slices of veal topped with prosciutto and sage, then sautéed in white wine and butter. The name "saltimbocca" means "jump in the mouth," reflecting the dish's burst of flavor.

Why try it?: A classic Roman main course that is simple, yet the combination of flavors from the veal, prosciutto, and sage is unforgettable.

Carciofi alla Romana. Roman-style artichokes, these are cooked in olive oil with garlic, mint, and parsley. The artichokes are typically stuffed and slowly braised until tender.

Why try it?: Artichokes are a staple of Roman cuisine, and this dish highlights their delicate flavor with a simple preparation that lets the vegetable shine.

Carciofi alla Giudia. This is a deep-fried version of artichokes, a famous dish from the Roman Jewish tradition. The artichokes are fried twice, resulting in a crispy, golden exterior with a tender inside.

Why try it?: A standout dish from Rome's Jewish ghetto, it's both a flavorful and historical experience for food lovers.

Trippa alla Romana. Roman-style tripe (the stomach lining of a cow) is slow-cooked in a tomato sauce with pecorino romano, garlic, and mint. It's a rich, hearty dish traditionally enjoyed by locals.

Why try it?: For adventurous eaters, this dish represents the Roman tradition of using every part of the animal, creating a rich and flavorful meal from humble ingredients.

Abbacchio alla Romana. This dish consists of roast lamb, often marinated with garlic, rosemary, and olive oil, then slow-cooked until tender and juicy. It's typically served with potatoes.

Why try it?: It's a favorite dish around Easter but is enjoyed year-round in Rome. The lamb is succulent and full of earthy flavors from the herbs.

Supplì (one of my favorites when in Rome!). A popular Roman street food, supplì are deep-fried rice balls typically stuffed with mozzarella and seasoned with tomato sauce. The crispy exterior gives way to a gooey, cheesy center.

Why try it?: Supplì are an indulgent snack or starter and are the Roman version of the more widely known Sicilian arancini.

Coda alla Vaccinara. A slow-cooked oxtail stew, simmered with tomatoes, celery, and wine. The oxtail is cooked until it's incredibly tender and flavorful.

Why try it?: It's a hearty, traditional dish that reflects Rome's working-class roots, perfect for cold days or for those wanting to experience authentic Roman comfort food.

Gnocchi alla Romana. Unlike the more common potato-based gnocchi, Roman gnocchi are made from semolina flour. The dough is shaped into discs, baked with butter and parmesan cheese, resulting in a golden, crispy top and a creamy center.

Why try it?: This dish offers a different take on gnocchi, unique to Rome and rich with buttery, cheesy flavors.

Maritozzo (Breakfast favorite, it is okay to order two of them!) A traditional Roman pastry, maritozzo is a soft, sweet bun filled with whipped cream. Historically, it was often given to brides-to-be by their grooms.

Why try it?: Maritozzo is a beloved Roman dessert, perfect for breakfast or as a sweet treat during a day of sightseeing.

Puntarelle. A type of chicory, puntarelle is a popular Roman salad ingredient, typically served with an anchovy, garlic, and vinegar dressing.

Why try it?: Puntarelle has a distinctive crunch and a slightly bitter taste, perfectly balanced by the salty, tangy anchovy dressing, making it a must-try Roman side dish.

Porchetta. Although originally from the countryside outside of Rome, porchetta (roasted pork) is incredibly popular in Roman cuisine. It is seasoned with garlic, rosemary, and other herbs, then roasted until the skin is crispy and the meat is tender.

Why try it?: Porchetta sandwiches are a common sight at Roman markets and food stalls, and they are delicious, savory, and satisfying.

Tiramisu. Although it originated in northern Italy, tiramisu is a favorite dessert in Rome. It's made from layers of coffee-soaked ladyfingers, mascarpone cheese, and cocoa powder.

Why try it?: Tiramisu is an iconic Italian dessert, and in Rome, you'll find excellent versions of this creamy, coffee flavored delight.

Bonus: Pizza al Taglio

Pizza al taglio (pizza by the slice) is a Roman invention, where pizza is baked in large rectangular trays and sold by weight. Toppings can range from classic margherita to more elaborate combinations.

Why try it?: It's a convenient and delicious way to enjoy pizza while exploring the city, with endless topping possibilities and a crispy yet chewy crust typical of Roman pizza.

These dishes reflect Rome's rich culinary tradition, showcasing its ability to take simple ingredients and elevate them into extraordinary flavors. When in Rome, trying these iconic dishes is essential to experiencing the city's culture!

Dining Recommendations by Area

Restaurants Near Piazza Navona

Da Francesco. Address: Piazza del Fico, 29. Known for its traditional Roman cuisine, Da Francesco is famous for its pizza and pasta dishes. It's a cozy, local favorite that draws both tourists and Romans for its authentic flavors and welcoming atmosphere.

Cul de Sac. Address: Piazza di Pasquino, 73. One of Rome's oldest wine bars, Cul de Sac offers a vast selection of Italian wines paired with regional dishes. Its cozy, informal setting makes it ideal for sampling local specialties like Roman-style tripe and pasta dishes.

Pizzeria Da Baffetto. Address: Via del Governo Vecchio, 114. A Roman institution, Da Baffetto is famous for its thin-crust pizzas. Be prepared for a lively, bustling atmosphere, as the restaurant is popular with both locals and visitors seeking classic Roman pizza.

Restaurants Near the Spanish Steps

Il Gabriello. Address: Via Vittoria, 51. Il Gabriello is a hidden gem offering a refined take on traditional Roman cuisine. Known for its cozy, elegant ambiance, the restaurant serves dishes like tonnarelli cacio e pepe and fresh seafood.

Ristorante Nino. Address: Via Borgognona, 11. A Roman classic, Nino is a traditional trattoria offering Tuscan-influenced Roman dishes. Famous for its bistecca alla fiorentina and handmade pastas, it's a long-standing favorite near the Spanish Steps.

Hostaria Romana. Address: Via del Boccaccio, 1. This restaurant offers classic Roman dishes like cacio e pepe and saltimbocca. Known for its friendly service and lively atmosphere, Hostaria Romana provides a true Roman dining experience.

Restaurants Near the Vatican

Ristorante Arlu (this is my favorite in the area. I visit EVERY trip!). Address: Borgo Pio, 135. Located just a short walk from St. Peter's Basilica, Arlu is a family-run restaurant serving Roman classics with a modern twist. Known for its friendly service and cozy atmosphere, it offers fresh pasta, meat dishes, and excellent desserts.

La Zanzara. Address: Via Crescenzio, 84. A trendy bistro near the Vatican, La Zanzara offers a mix of traditional Italian dishes and creative cuisine. Popular with both locals and tourists, it's known for its lively ambiance, pizza, and regional Roman dishes.

Hostaria Dino e Toni. Address: Via Leone IV, 60. A classic Roman trattoria known for its generous portions and lively atmosphere. Dino e Toni serves traditional Roman dishes, such as carbonara, amatriciana, and hearty meat dishes, in a family-style setting.

Taverna Angelica. Address: Piazza Americo Capponi, 6. This elegant restaurant near the Vatican is known for its sophisticated Roman and Mediterranean cuisine. Taverna Angelica offers a seasonal menu that emphasizes fresh ingredients, including homemade pasta and seafood.

Restaurants in Trastevere

Da Enzo al 29 (My favorite in the area. Consistently delicious!). Address: Via dei Vascellari, 29. A small, family-run trattoria in Trastevere known for its authentic Roman cuisine. Da Enzo serves traditional dishes like carbonara, amatriciana, and oxtail, made with fresh, local ingredients. The cozy setting and friendly service make it a must-visit.

Osteria der Belli. Address: Piazza di Sant'Apollonia, 11A. A local favorite offering traditional Roman and Sardinian cuisine. Known for its fresh seafood and homemade pasta, Osteria der Belli is a charming spot to enjoy authentic Italian flavors in a relaxed setting.

Trattoria da Teo. Address: Piazza dei Ponziani, 7A. Famous for its seasonal dishes and traditional Roman fare, Trattoria da Teo is in a quieter part of Trastevere. Its menu includes fresh artichokes, homemade pasta, and daily specials, all served in a warm, rustic atmosphere.

Antica Trattoria Da Carlone. Address: Via della Luce, 5. A traditional Roman trattoria known for its rich and flavorful pasta dishes, especially the carbonara and cacio e pepe. The generous portions and friendly service make it a popular spot for both locals and visitors.

Tonnarello. Address: Via della Paglia, 1. One of the busiest and most beloved spots in Trastevere, Tonnarello serves classic Roman cuisine, with standout dishes like cacio e pepe and gnocchi. Its lively atmosphere and generous portions keep both tourists and locals coming back.

Restaurants Near the Pantheon

Armando al Pantheon. Address: Salita dei Crescenzi, 31. A historic restaurant just steps from the Pantheon, Armando al Pantheon offers traditional Roman dishes with a focus on quality ingredients. The menu includes classic Roman pastas and hearty meat dishes, all served in an intimate setting.

Da Fortunato al Pantheon. Address: Via del Pantheon, 55. Known for its elegant ambiance and excellent Roman cuisine, Da Fortunato al Pantheon has been serving guests for decades. The restaurant specializes in Roman classics like saltimbocca and amatriciana, and also offers a fine selection of wines.

Ristorante Alfredo alla Scrofa. Address: Via della Scrofa, 104. Famous for creating the original "Fettuccine Alfredo," this historic restaurant near the Pantheon is a must-visit for fans of classic Italian dishes. The elegant interior and timeless menu make it a popular choice for a special night out.

Il Bacaro. Address: Via degli Spagnoli, 27. A small, intimate restaurant offering a blend of Roman and Tuscan cuisine. Il Bacaro is known for its fresh, seasonal ingredients and cozy, romantic atmosphere. It's the go-to spot for a romantic dinner near the Pantheon.

Ristorante La Tavernetta 48. Address: Via degli Spagnoli, 48. A cozy and traditional Roman trattoria offering hearty Roman dishes like rigatoni alla carbonara, cacio e pepe, and saltimbocca. Known for its welcoming service and homey atmosphere, it's a superb choice for a classic Roman meal in the center of the city.

Pasticcerie (Bakeries) and Coffee Recommendations by Area

Forget "When in Rome, do as the Romans do" - I've discovered my own eternal city survival guide: Follow the flour! While others chase Michelin stars, I've realized I could sustain myself purely on Rome's pasticcerie. Who needs a dinner reservation when you can have a delicious experience with a maritozzo? Let the tourists fight over restaurant tables - I'll be staging my own Roman holiday, leaving a trail of powdered sugar from one bakery to the next.

Pasticcerie and Coffee Near Campo de' Fiori

Roscioli Caffè Pasticceria (My favorite Pasticceria!). Address: Piazza Benedetto Cairoli, 16. A local favorite, Roscioli offers both a bakery and coffee shop experience. Known for its artisanal breads, pastries, and top-quality espressos, Roscioli is a must-stop for anyone visiting the Campo de' Fiori area. Don't miss their famous maritozzi (Roman cream buns) or their selection of cornetti, perfect with a cappuccino. Signature Item: Make sure and try their Maritozzo!!

Forno Campo de' Fiori. Address: Piazza Campo de' Fiori, 22. A historic bakery just off the famous Campo de' Fiori market, this spot is known for its pizza bianca but also serves excellent pastries and coffee. It's perfect for a morning espresso and something sweet, like biscotti or their freshly baked bread.

Sant'Eustachio Il Caffè (My favorite coffee in Rome. I buy bags to bring home.) Address: Piazza di Sant'Eustachio, 82. Famous for its signature creamy espresso, Sant'Eustachio has been serving coffee in Rome since

1938. It's a brilliant spot to enjoy a traditional Italian coffee alongside a pastry like a cornetto or a ciambella.

Pasticcerie and Coffee Near the Spanish Steps

Antico Caffè Greco. Address: Via dei Condotti, 86. Established in 1760, Antico Caffè Greco is one of Rome's oldest coffeehouses. It's famous for its classic espresso served in a charming, historic setting. The pasticceria here offers traditional pastries to pair with your coffee, perfect for an elegant Roman experience.

Ciampini Roma. Address: Piazza di San Lorenzo in Lucina, 29. Known for its gelato and pastries, Ciampini offers a sophisticated atmosphere near the Spanish Steps. Whether it's a croissant in the morning or a sweet tart in the afternoon, their selection of treats and expertly made coffee will enhance any visit to the area.

Pasticceria D'Angelo. Address: Via della Croce, 10. A family-run pasticceria located near the Spanish Steps, D'Angelo is known for its delicious variety of sweets, including tiramisu, cornetti, and cannoli.

Pasticcerie and Coffee Near the Vatican

Sciascia Caffè 1919. Address: Via Fabio Massimo, 80/A. Known for its exquisite espresso and vintage atmosphere, Sciascia Caffè is a hidden gem near the Vatican. It's a great spot for a quiet break with a traditional Italian pastry and a cup of their famous rich coffee.

Pasticceria Bonci. Address: Via della Meloria, 83. Famous for its artisan bread and pastries, Bonci is a favorite stop for those seeking high-quality baked goods near the Vatican. Their cakes and biscuits are top-notch, and their cornetti are perfect with an espresso for breakfast.

Pasticcerie and Coffee in Trastevere

Pasticceria Valzani. Address: Via del Moro, 37a. Valzani is a family-run pasticceria that has been serving up sweets since 1925. Famous for its traditional Roman pastries like torrone and panpepato, this shop is perfect for those looking for authentic flavors in a historic setting.

Bar San Calisto. Address: Piazza di San Calisto, 3. A classic Roman bar where you can enjoy coffee, pastries, and gelato. San Calisto is an affordable and authentic spot to soak in the local culture while sipping on espresso and enjoying a sweet treat.

Pasticceria Trastevere. Address: Via Natale del Grande, 50. A neighborhood favorite, Pasticceria Trastevere offers an array of Roman sweets and freshly made pastries. Whether you're in the mood for a simple cornetto or a rich tiramisu, this shop provides a delicious selection in a friendly, casual atmosphere.

CHAPTER TWENTY-FOUR

Accommodation Detail

Types of Accommodation and Recommendations by Area

Hotel Star Ratings Explained

Hotel star ratings provide travelers with a quick reference to gauge the quality and services offered by a hotel. These ratings are typically assigned by local tourism boards or international hotel associations, and while they can vary slightly depending on the country, the basic principles are generally the same.

1-Star Hotels. A 1-star hotel offers the most basic accommodations. These hotels typically provide minimal services and facilities, such as: Clean, functional rooms. Basic amenities, like a bed, a bathroom, and simple furnishings. Daily housekeeping.

Very limited additional services (e.g., no restaurant or 24-hour reception). Budget-friendly options, perfect for travelers who simply need a place to sleep without extra frills.

2-Star Hotels. A 2-star hotel offers slightly more comfort than a 1-star property. You can expect: Clean, slightly more spacious rooms with basic amenities. A TV, phone, and often an en-suite bathroom. Limited on-site services, such as breakfast or a small café.

Wi-Fi availability, though it may not always be free. These hotels cater to budget-conscious travelers seeking basic, but slightly enhanced, facilities.

3-Star Hotels. A 3-star hotel balances comfort and affordability, offering more amenities and services, including: Comfortable rooms with more furniture, such as a desk or seating area. On-site dining

options (such as a restaurant or bar). 24-hour reception service but may not be onsite.

Additional services like room service, laundry, and parking. Fitness centers or small pools may be available. A 3-star hotel is typically ideal for travelers seeking a mid-range option with adequate comfort and convenience.

4-Star Hotels. A 4-star hotel offers a more upscale experience with a wide range of amenities and high-quality services.

Expect: Spacious, well-decorated rooms with modern furnishings. Multiple dining options, including a fine-dining restaurant. Enhanced facilities such as fitness centers, spas, pools, and business services.

Concierge services, valet parking, and 24-hour room service. These hotels cater to travelers who want a more luxurious experience without the cost of a 5-star property.

5-Star Hotels. The highest standard of luxury, a 5-star hotel provides world-class services and facilities. Typically, you can expect: Large, luxurious rooms with high-end furnishings, premium bedding, and state-of-the-art technology.

Multiple upscale dining options, including gourmet restaurants. Extensive facilities, such as full-service spas, fitness centers, pools, and sometimes even golf courses. Personalized services like concierge, butler service, and private transfers.

Attention to detail in service, décor, and overall experience. These hotels are designed for guests seeking the pinnacle of comfort, style, and service.

Luxury and Beyond

Some hotels go beyond 5 stars and are considered luxury, boutique, or ultra-luxury properties. These hotels provide exceptionally personalized services, often in unique or exclusive settings. They might be small boutique hotels offering custom experiences or part of renowned global luxury hotel brands.

Hotels by Area

Due to Rome's size and diverse neighborhoods, finding the perfect hotel or apartment can be difficult with a simple map search. Instead, I recommend using Booking.com if you're looking for hotels or Airbnb for apartments. Both platforms offer easy-to-use map tools that allow you to focus on specific areas of Rome and filter by price per night, helping you find the best accommodation that fits your budget and location preferences.

When using these platforms, it's helpful to understand hotel star ratings, which give travelers a general sense of what to expect in terms of comfort, services, and amenities. A higher star rating typically means more amenities and personalized services, but choosing the right hotel depends on your travel style and budget. Use Booking.com to compare ratings and amenities for hotels, or Airbnb.com to explore apartments with more space and flexibility for longer stays.

Hotels Near Piazza Navona (this is my preferred area to stay when in Rome)

Hotel Raphael – Relais & Châteaux (5 stars). Address: Largo Febo, 2

A luxury eco-friendly hotel offering an impressive rooftop terrace with panoramic views of the city. The hotel features elegant rooms, suites with designer furnishings, and a focus on sustainability. It is located just a short walk from Piazza Navona and offers a blend of luxury and sustainability.

Hotel Genio (4 stars). Address: Via Giuseppe Zanardelli, 28

Located right in the center of Rome, Hotel Genio offers classical Roman architecture and a rooftop terrace with stunning views of Piazza Navona and St. Peter's Basilica. This elegant hotel is a fantastic option for travelers wanting proximity to Rome's most famous piazzas and landmarks.

Navona Theater Hotel (3 stars). Address: Vicolo dei Granari, 3

This is where I stayed my last visit, very nice. This boutique 3-star hotel is a cozy and modern accommodation option in the centro storico. Its contemporary design and convenient location just 1 minute from Piazza Navona make it ideal for visitors looking for style and comfort without breaking the bank.

Hotels Near the Spanish Steps

Hotel d'Inghilterra Roma–Starhotels Collezione (5 stars). Address: Via Bocca di Leone, 14

A luxurious hotel located just steps from the Spanish Steps and Via Condotti. This historic hotel is renowned for its refined style and blend of classic Roman elegance and modern comfort. It's perfect for those wanting to immerse themselves in Rome's upscale shopping and historic sites.

Hotel Condotti (4 stars). Address: Via Mario de' Fiori, 37

This charming boutique hotel is located right by the Spanish Steps and Via Condotti, one of the best shopping streets in Rome. It offers an intimate atmosphere with modern comforts and personalized service, ideal for visitors wanting both comfort and proximity to major sites.

Hotel Scalinata di Spagna (3 stars). Address: Piazza della Trinità dei Monti, 17

This quaint 3-star hotel offers stunning views over Rome and is located just steps from the top of the Spanish Steps. Known for its cozy atmosphere, Scalinata di Spagna offers a warm and comfortable stay with all the major landmarks within walking distance.

Hotels Near the Vatican

Starhotels Michelangelo Rome (4 stars). Address: Via della Stazione di S. Pietro, 14

Just a few minutes' walk from St. Peter's Basilica, Starhotels Michelangelo combines modern comfort with traditional Roman style.

Hotel Paolo II (3 stars). Address: Via Paolo II, 3

A charming, budget-friendly option, Hotel Paolo II offers modern rooms in a peaceful area near the Vatican. Located in a historic building, it provides a quiet retreat from the hustle and bustle while being just minutes from St. Peter's Square.

Hotels in Trastevere

Donna Camilla Savelli Hotel (4 stars). Address: Via Garibaldi, 27

Housed in a 17th-century former convent, this beautiful 4-star hotel offers a serene garden, elegant rooms, and a fantastic location in the heart of Trastevere. It's perfect for those seeking tranquility while still being near Rome's bustling center.

Hotel Santa Maria (3 stars). Address: Vicolo del Piede, 2

A cozy and charming 3-star hotel, Hotel Santa Maria offers a peaceful escape with a beautiful courtyard garden in the heart of Trastevere. Its warm atmosphere and personalized service make it an ideal retreat for couples or families.

Hotel Ripa Roma (4 stars). Address: Via degli Orti di Trastevere, 3

A modern hotel in the lively Trastevere district, Hotel Ripa Roma offers contemporary design with spacious rooms. It's well-suited for travelers looking for a stylish and comfortable stay with easy access to Trastevere's vibrant dining and nightlife.

Hotels Near the Pantheon

Albergo del Senato (3 stars). Address: Piazza della Rotonda, 73

A classic Roman hotel with an unbeatable location directly in front of the Pantheon. Albergo del Senato offers elegant rooms, a rooftop terrace, and traditional charm, perfect for those looking to stay in the heart of historic Rome.

Grand Hotel De La Minerve (5 stars). Address: Piazza della Minerva, 69

A luxury 5-star hotel offering a perfect blend of classic elegance and modern amenities. Located just steps from the Pantheon, this historic hotel boasts a rooftop terrace with panoramic views, ideal for travelers seeking a lavish experience.

Hotel Abruzzi (3 stars). Address: Piazza della Rotonda, 69

Offering stunning views of the Pantheon from many rooms, this charming 3-star hotel is perfect for those wanting a central location. Perfect for travelers who desire to wake up to Rome's iconic sites.

Chapter Twenty-Five

Flexible and Walkable Itineraries

Maximize your time in Rome

Rome is a city best discovered on foot, where every cobblestone street holds surprises. These itineraries are designed to maximize your time by grouping nearby sites together, minimizing travel time, and including strategic breaks. Whether you're here for 3, 5, or 8 nights during the 2025 Jubilee Year, you'll experience Rome's spiritual and cultural treasures while walking efficiently between locations.

Three-Night Essential Rome

(Optimized for minimal travel time between major sites)

Day 1: Vatican & Prati District
Morning:

- Start early at St. Peter's Basilica (opens 7 AM) before crowds arrive

- Holy Door pilgrimage, Pietà, and Baldacchino

- Dome climb for morning views (recommended before it gets hot)

- Pro tip: Enter through the security line near the Vatican post office for shorter queues

Afternoon:

- Vatican Museums and Sistine Chapel (book tickets for 2 PM to avoid peak crowds)

- Consider "skip-the-line" tickets to maximize time

- Walking route: Exit through Porta Sant'Anna to explore the elegant Prati neighborhood

Evening:

- Sunset stroll through Borgo Pio

- Dinner at Ristorante Arlu (5-minute walk from St. Peter's)

- Night photos of illuminated St. Peter's Square

Day 2: Ancient Rome & Jewish Quarter
(All sites within a 20-minute walking radius)

Morning:

- Start at Colosseum (book first entry at 8:30 AM)

- Roman Forum (natural progression from Colosseum)

- Walking route: Exit Forum through Capitol Hill

Afternoon:

- Jewish Ghetto for lunch

- Turtle Fountain

- Walk to nearby Basilica of San Clemente (3-tiered church showing Rome's layers)

- Transportation tip: If tired, bus 87 connects Colosseum to Jewish Quarter

Evening:

- Campo de' Fiori for aperitivo

- Dinner in Trastevere (cross Ponte Sisto for scenic river views)

Day 3: Historic Center Loop
(Circular walking route connecting major basilicas)

Morning:

- Begin at Basilica of St. Mary Major

- Walk to St. John Lateran (15 minutes)

- Visit Holy Stairs (adjacent to basilica)

Afternoon:

- Pantheon area for lunch

- Walking loop: Piazza Navona → Church of Sant'Agnese → Sant'Andrea della Valle

- End at stunning Aventine Hill for sunset views

Evening:

- Farewell dinner near Piazza Navona

- Night walk through illuminated historic center

Five-Night Rome Experience

(Balanced pilgrimage and cultural exploration)

Day 1: Vatican Immersion
Morning:

- 7 AM: St. Peter's Basilica (beat tour groups)

- Holy Door pilgrimage and Crypt

- Dome climb in cool morning hours

- Pro tip: Book Scavi tour in advance for 10:30 AM slot

Afternoon:

- 2 PM: Vatican Museums (crowds typically lighter)

- Exit through Sistine Chapel to St. Peter's to save 30 minutes walking

- Transportation tip: Metro to Cipro station for museum entrance, exit near St. Peter's

Evening:

- Explore Borgo and Prati neighborhoods

- Dinner near Castel Sant'Angelo for night views

Day 2: Ancient Christian Rome Loop
(Eastern basilicas connected by efficient walking route)

Morning:

- Start at St. John Lateran

- Holy Stairs and Baptistry

- Short walk to Holy Cross in Jerusalem

- Walking tip: Use tree-lined Via Carlo Felice between basilicas

Afternoon:

- St. Mary Major

- Santa Prassede (hidden gem 5 minutes away)

- Transportation tip: Bus 40 Express back to center

Evening:

- Monti neighborhood for dinner

- Stroll past illuminated Trajan's Column

Day 3: Underground Rome
Morning:

- Catacombs of San Callisto (take first tour)

- Appian Way walking experience

- Transportation tip: Bus 118 from Circo Massimo station

Afternoon:

- San Clemente Basilica (walking down through three levels of Rome)

- Continue to Colosseum area

- Forum walk through to Capitol Hill

Evening:

- Sunset from Campidoglio

- Dinner in Jewish Ghetto

Day 4: Historic Center Spiritual Walk
(Circular route connecting major churches)

Morning:

- Start at Pantheon (opens early)

- Santa Maria Sopra Minerva

- Sant'Ignazio (10-minute walk)

- Walking tip: Use small alleys for shade

Afternoon:

- Piazza Navona area churches

- Chiesa Nuova

- Cross river to Trastevere

Evening:

- Santa Maria in Trastevere

- Dinner in Trastevere's quieter streets

Day 5: Art and Reflection
Morning:

- Early entry Borghese Gallery (must book ahead)

- Villa Borghese Gardens walk

- Santa Maria della Vittoria (Bernini's masterpiece)

Afternoon:

- Spanish Steps area

- Trinità dei Monti

- Shopping break on Via Condotti

Evening:

- Farewell dinner near Trevi Fountain

- Night fountain walk through historic center

Eight-Night Comprehensive Stay

(Rome in depth, countryside, and hidden gems)

Days 1-5 follow five-night itinerary above, then continue with:

Day 6: Museum Day & Hidden Churches
Morning:

- Capitoline Museums

- Mamertine Prison

- Santa Maria in Aracoeli

Afternoon:

- Palazzo Doria Pamphilj

- Hidden churches walk: San Luigi dei Francesi (Caravaggio) → Sant'Agostino → San Giovanni dei Fiorentini

- Walking tip: Use Via dei Coronari for scenic route

Evening:

- Dinner in Campo de' Fiori

- Night walk through Jewish Ghetto

Day 7: Castel Gandolfo Excursion
Early train to Castel Gandolfo

- Apostolic Palace tour

- Papal Gardens

- Transportation tip: Book combo ticket with train included

Afternoon:

- Explore Albano Laziale

- Wine tasting in Frascati

- Optional: Visit Ariccia for famous porchetta

Evening:

- Return to Rome

- Dinner along Tiber River

Day 8: Off-the-Beaten-Path Rome
Morning:

- Aventine Hill churches

- Orange Garden view

- Rose Garden (in season)

- Walking tip: Follow the Clivo di Rocca Savella down

Afternoon:

- Testaccio food exploration

- Protestant Cemetery

- Villa Farnesina (Raphael frescoes)

Evening:

- Final dinner in Trastevere

- Night walk across Rome's bridges

Additional Tips for All Itineraries:

- Purchase Roma Pass for primary sites

- Use metro for longer distances (especially Vatican to Eastern basilicas)

- Schedule indoor activities during peak heat (12-3 PM)

- Carry water bottle (Rome has drinking fountains everywhere)

- Book major sites online to avoid queues

- Consider early morning or evening visits to outdoor sites in summer

- Look for "secret" passageways between sites (like the passage from Palazzo Colonna to Via Nazionale)

CHAPTER TWENTY-SIX

Reflections on the Jubilee Year

A Journey of Faith, Hope, and Renewal

A s the Jubilee Year 2025 draws to a close, we find ourselves at the end of an extraordinary journey of faith, hope, and renewal. From the opening of the Holy Doors on Christmas Eve 2024 to the final celebrations in December 2025, millions of pilgrims from around the world have walked the paths of Rome, seeking spiritual renewal and experiencing the universal embrace of the Church.

A Year of Celebrations

Throughout this Jubilee Year, Rome has been a focal point of faith, hosting a diverse array of events that have touched every facet of the Church and human experience.

These events testify to the Church's dedication in providing a welcoming and renewing home for everyone, regardless of their circumstances.

The Power of Pilgrimage

The heart of the Jubilee experience has been the pilgrimage - a physical journey that mirrors an inner spiritual transformation. Millions have walked through the Holy Doors of Rome's major basilicas, each step a prayer, each passage a symbol of moving from sin to grace, from the old self to the new.

The Giro delle Sette Chiese revived for this Jubilee, has allowed pilgrims to connect with centuries of tradition, walking in the footsteps of saints like Philip Neri. The journey through Rome's sacred heart has powerfully reminded us of faith's unbroken continuity.

Faith in a Digital Age

The Jubilee of 2025 has also showcased the Church's engagement with the modern world. Events like the Jubilee of Digital Missionaries and Catholic Influencers have highlighted new frontiers of evangelization. The focus on environmental stewardship throughout the celebrations has underscored the Church's commitment to care for our common home.

Technology, like the Carta del Pellegrino, has improved the Jubilee, making it more accessible and organized without losing its spiritual essence.

Renewal and Hope

The theme "Pilgrims of Hope" has resonated throughout the year, offering a message of encouragement and renewal to a world facing numerous challenges. In times of uncertainty, the Jubilee stands as a beacon of hope, reminding us of the lasting strength found in faith and community.

Emphasizing mercy and reconciliation, especially in events like the Jubilee of Consolation and Jubilee of Prisoners, serves as a powerful testament to God's love's ability to transform.

The Journey Continues

The 2025 Jubilee will be remembered for more than just grand celebrations and the participation of millions. It will also be remembered for the countless personal stories of renewal, reconciliation, and recommitment to faith. It has been a year of encountering Christ in new and profound ways - in the sacraments, in sacred spaces, in acts of charity, and the faces of our fellow pilgrims.

As we step forward from this Jubilee Year, may we do so as true "Pilgrims of Hope," bearing witness to the transformative power of faith and carrying the light of Christ into every corner of our world. The journey of faith continues, enriched by the experiences of this extraordinary year and strengthened by the bonds of our global Catholic community.

In the words of Pope Francis, as we conclude this Jubilee, let us remember: "Hope never disappoints. Optimism disappoints, but hope does not!" May the hope kindled in this Jubilee Year burn brightly in our hearts, illuminating our path forward and inspiring us to build a more just, compassionate, and faith-filled world.

A Personal Invitation

I look forward to sharing the 2025 Jubilee experience with you. This promises to be an extraordinary time of faith, renewal, and community. Should you have the chance to join any events, I'd be delighted to share your experience. Please tag me in your Instagram posts while you are in Rome! @katerinaferraraauthor.

Feel free to reach out and share your stories, reflections, and the impact these moments have had on your faith journey.

May your Jubilee journey be filled with moments of grace, joy, and profound spiritual renewal.

CHAPTER TWENTY-SEVEN

Select Bibliography

And Recommended Reading

B roers, Michael. Napoleon: The Spirit of the Age, 1805-1810. Faber & Faber, 2018.

Furet, François. Napoleon and the Transformation of Europe. Harvard University Press, 1990.

Hibbard, Howard. Michelangelo: Painter, Sculptor, Architect. Harper & Row, 1974.

Langdon, Helen. Caravaggio: A Life. Farrar, Straus and Giroux, 1998.

Scotti, R.A. Basilica: The Splendor and the Scandal: Building St. Peter's. New York: Viking, 2006. - **Recommended Reading.**

Wittkower, Rudolf. Bernini: The Sculptor of the Roman Baroque. Phaidon Press, 1955.

Photography: All photographs are my own.

Thank You & Please Leave a Review

Thank you for reading this book in the Travel Italy Series

If the guide enhanced your travel planning, I'd greatly appreciate it if you could leave a review on Amazon. Your feedback not only helps other travelers, but also supports this book's success.

Scan Here

I would love to hear about your own adventures! Connect with me on Instagram, where I share hundreds of videos from the festivals of Sicily and Italy—perfect for a sneak peek before your trip.

For even more travel inspiration, visit my blog for deeper dives into Italy's stunning beaches and off-the-beaten-path gems, which are not covered extensively in this guide. https://katerinaferrara.com/blog/

Thank you for being part of this journey, and I look forward to hearing about yours!

Wishing you the safest and happiest travels!

Katerina Ferrara

Connect with Me

Free Italy Travel Resources and More

Newsletter / Travel News

Sign up for my newsletter and stay updated with insider secrets about Italy's charming towns, vibrant festivals, and mouthwatering food—things you won't find in any travel guide. Stay updated with the latest on festivals, tours, podcasts, and special insights that go beyond the book!

Link to KaterinaFerra ra.com

Immersion Travel by Katerina Ferrara Blog

Looking for even more hidden gems in Italy? My blog is packed with insider tips, from secret beaches tucked away on Italy's lesser-known coastlines to self-guided walking tours that take you off the typical tourist path. Whether you're planning a relaxing escape or an adventurous exploration, you'll find everything you need to create unforgettable Italian journeys. Subscribe at for exclusive travel insights and start uncovering Italy's best-kept secrets! www.katerinaferrara.com

Stay Connected

Follow me on social media to see the festivals of Italy as they come to life every day of the year and tag me in your posts when you visit Rome.

Instagram: @KaterinaFerraraAuthor

Festival Enthusiasts - Immersion Travel Italy offers one-of-a-kind experiences for travelers seeking to connect deeply with Italy's culture. We organize small-group journeys to discover Italy's most vibrant festivals and sagre, explore charming towns, and embark on unforgettable adventures. Whether you're savoring local delicacies at a food festival or taking part in centuries-old traditions, our personalized trips allow you to experience the heart and soul of Italy like a local. Join us for an immersive travel experience you'll treasure forever!

Corrections / Updates / Suggestions Oops!

Even the best of us can make mistakes. I would appreciate your help to make my content better. Please visit the book page here: https://katerinaferrara.com/2025-jubilee-year-guide/and scroll down to the book feedback button.

Katerina Ferrara

About the Author

Katerina Ferrara is a published author and the founder of Immersion Travel Italy, a company dedicated to creating unforgettable travel experiences in Italy. With over 25 years of exploring Europe, Katerina has developed a deep love for immersing herself in the diverse cultures, traditions, and culinary delights of the places she visits. Fluent in Italian, she effortlessly connects with locals and travelers alike, bringing an insider's perspective to her travel writing.

Katerina jokes that she lives her life on a perpetual diet—not for vanity, but to prepare for the next irresistible festival in Italy. Her ultimate dream is to inspire **Festival Followers**—travelers who prioritize experiencing incredible festivals first and then explore the surrounding sites while immersing themselves in local traditions. She believes festivals offer a unique lens into a region's heart and culture, making them the perfect starting point for any adventure.

An avid hiker and fitness enthusiast, Katerina incorporates her passion for staying active into her travels, often seeking out scenic trails, walking tours, and outdoor adventures that connect her to the natural beauty of a destination (while making room for just a little more gelato).

When she's not exploring new destinations or writing, Katerina enjoys sharing her travel insights and tips with fellow adventurers, inspiring them to delve deeper into the cultural richness of the places they visit—and maybe even discover their own favorite festival.

www.ingramcontent.com/pod-product-compliance
Lightning Source LLC
Chambersburg PA
CBHW060922120626
46557CB00003B/848